The De Loreans: Why did Cristina split?

Diana Ross, Ron vs. Fritz, Amadeus & the Queen's dressmaker

People weekly

The remarkable true story behind FARRAH'S SHOCKER

On the night of March 9, 1977, Michigan housewife Francine Hughes, who had been brutally beaten by her husband for years, decided she had had enough. As he lay sleeping, she poured gasoline around his bed, dropped a match and left him to die in flames. To some people it seemed a clear-cut case of murder, to others no more than justice for his relentless cruelty. Next week Farrah Fawcett (left) brings the drama to T.V. Here, for the first time, is the full account of what has happened to Francine and her family since that awful night.

Oprah goes Hollywood for a 40th-birthday bash

People weekly

TONYA'S WORLD

As Tonya Harding fights for her future—and possibly her freedom—her parents and friends describe the hard life that shaped her

Ex-husband Jeff Gillooly (above) says Harding helped plot the attack on rival skater Nancy Kerrigan

---

The shocking story of the Born Free murder

People weekly

The Fall of Queen Leona

GUILTY! GUILTY! GUILTY!

Why did one of the world's richest women chisel pennies off her taxes? As LEONA HELMSLEY faces years in prison, those closest to her describe a fearful, insecure person who grew up poor and could never get rich enough

---

People

Nicole Simpson & Ron Goldman

THE FORGOTTEN VICTIMS

Police say O.J. Simpson brutally murdered two people in the prime of their lives. Here are their stories

---

The Canadian skaters: A fiery love story

David Pelletier & Jamie Salé

People weekly

After bouts with mental illness, ANDREA YATES drowned her five children. Now a jury must decide:

VILLAIN OR VICTIM?

The Yates family in November 2000, prior to Mary's birth (Clockwise from top right: Rusty, Noah, Paul, Luke, John and Andrea). Far right, Andrea at a hearing last June

---

Bruce, Tracy, Sting & friends hit the road for human rights

People weekly

A CRY FOR HELP

Fearing for her life, friends of Robin Givens leak a frightening story of Mike Tyson's private violence and his threat to kill them both

---

Van Damme's (fourth) divorce • Meet the new Brady Bunch

People weekly

DEATH OF A MADMAN

The revealing last days and violent death of JEFFREY DAHMER, America's most notorious killer

---

CHELSEA CLINTON: Out of the White House, into the dorm

People weekly

MOM & DAD UNDER SUSPICION

WHO ARE JOHN AND PATSY RAMSEY?

Nine months after the murder of 6-year-old JONBENET, family, friends and neighbors paint conflicting portraits of the couple at the heart of a terrible mystery

The Ramseys asserted their innocence in a May interview

Hunk and circumstance: Joey Lawrence graduates

People weekly

The Nicole Simpson Murders

LOVE AND DEATH

The shocking story of the volatile, violent relationship between O. J. Simpson and his beautiful ex-wife

O. J. and Nicole with daughter Sydney in 1986. Simpson's body (inset) is removed from the scene where she and Ronald Goldman were slain last week

---

The friends from Friends: TV's hottest new faces

People weekly

A rising pop star is murdered at 23

THE DEATH OF SELENA

Grammy-winning singer Selena was shot and killed by the former president of her fan club in Texas

---

A TV star finds his unknown daughter

Northern Exposure's Barry Corbin

People weekly

LETHAL LOLITA

Amy Fisher, 18, shot her alleged lover's wife—and unleashed a shocking tale of sex, greed and betrayal

AMY FISHER Was she a victim, too?

The real Jane Roe • Bon Jovi's bride • Cary Grant's ex • Katie Wagner

People weekly

The Central Park Outrage

NIGHT OF THE 'WILDING'

It was the ultimate urban nightmare. On a cool spring night a 28-year-old investment banker was out for her nightly jog in the park when as many as a dozen teenagers came out of the darkness. They could not escape—there were too many of them. They beat her savagely, raped her and left her for dead, their last casualty in a series of pack attacks that night. As their victim struggled for life, one of the suspects allegedly told police, "It was fun." Here is the story of a crime that shocked the nation—and roused a city to fury.

- Backstage with Mötley Crüe
- Women in combat

People weekly

The outrage in Boston

MURDER & DECEIT

Charles Stuart's claim that a black assailant killed his pregnant wife, Carol, shocked the nation; the deadly truth was even more terrible. Here is the story of a husband's treachery, a dark family secret and the inescapable guilt that led to suicide

Charles and Carol Stuart, insets; large photo, police pull Charles's body from the Mystic River after his fatal plunge from Boston's Tobin Bridge

---

A BALLERINA'S DEATH: STARVING FOR SUCCESS

Bill Cosby's courtroom revelations

Father or father figure?

Boston dancer Heidi Guenther

People weekly

MURDER OF A FASHION KING

The brazen shooting of designer to the stars GIANNI VERSACE sends the FBI on a frantic manhunt for a serial killer

Versace and client Cindy Crawford at a New York City benefit in 1992

WANTED: Andrew Cunanan

Dan Rather battles the heat (and NBC!) in the Middle East

People weekly

EXCLUSIVE

Lisa Steinberg's mother:

"THEY KILLED MY LITTLE GIRL"

Here is the untold story of Michele Launders's horrifying discovery that her child, illegally adopted by Joel Steinberg and Hedda Nussbaum, was the victim in the nation's most shocking child abuse case. Michele's agony had just begun...

Celebs frolic in Aspen • Motherhood after 60 • TV's Jerry Springer

People weekly

TERROR ON ICE

THE BIZARRE PLOT AGAINST NANCY KERRIGAN

EXCLUSIVE At home with the injured skater as she renews her quest for Olympic gold

Reports linked slain Tonya Harding's bodyguard Shawn Eckardt to the attack on Kerrigan

---

LOPEZ IN LOVE: Jennifer and her dancer get engaged

SPECIAL SECTION

CELEBRITY DIET & FITNESS

MADONNA & family: A burglar in the house

Tom Cruise's 39th birthday bash

Drew Barrymore weds (really)!

People

People

TRUE CRIME STORIES
CASES THAT SHOCKED AMERICA

CRIME IN OUR TIME

I N 31 YEARS PEOPLE HAS RUN 123 COVER STORIES ABOUT CRIME. INSIDE we've published hundreds more, about villains, victims, grifters, frauds, scheming sons, stalkers, greedy magnates, socialites with automatic weapons, bigamists, burglars, matricidal maniacs, women scorned, poisoners, plotters, cannibals, murderous gurus, killer Yuppies, sex-crazed scions and exactly one (1) blind bank robber.

In the process we've learned two things: The covers are often best-sellers, and the inside stories are among the best-read.

Why? Crime is news; something happened. Often it happened to someone just like us—it's scary. Or it happened to someone not at all like us—someone rich and famous—and opens a window on a private world. There are questions to answer, clues to follow, a trial to watch unfold. Some stories remain mysteries; some, when the evil perp gets sent to jail, become reassuring morality tales. In every case, though, something dramatic happened to a human being—which makes the story interesting to PEOPLE, and people.

Here are some of the best from the past three decades.

CONTENTS

by Scott Turow

I HAVE MADE A LIFE OF CRIME

—NOT IN THE SENSE THAT I'VE EVER REACHED FOR A MASK AND GUN, but rather as someone who for years has found crime the centerpiece of most of the work I do. My novels usually revolve around the who and the why of particular offenses—murder, fraud and bribery, generally speaking, which are the same crimes that have preoccupied me as a lawyer for more than a quarter of a century, first as a prosecutor and now as a defense attorney.

I had been largely blind to the fierce hold crime had on my imagination until I became a supervisor in the U.S. Attorney's Office in Chicago in the early 1980s. At that point I was a wannabe novelist who had gone to law school rather than continue to write unpublished novels, as I had done for five years after college. As a supervising prosecutor, I discovered that going up to court to observe the trials of the younger lawyers I was in charge of was not as simple as I had anticipated. Usually I visited at the high point of the prosecution case, when the government's chief witness was on the stand. But once I was in the courtroom, I couldn't leave. I was virtually cemented to my seat by the witness's account

How many people do you know who *didn't* interrupt their day to watch the O.J. verdict? Anybody out there who can raise their right hand and say they've never speculated about who really killed JonBenét Ramsey?

Given my own fascination, I have often asked myself why acts of evil are so spellbinding. Why are crimes, cops and trials so compelling? I'd venture several answers. First, crimes reveal some of our deepest anxieties about the risks of everyday life. We all depend, each day, on people we don't know: We count on strangers not to run us down in the cross-walk, break into our homes, or assault us on the street. When those things happen, they touch on our most primitive fears. In part, the murder of Gianni Ver-

eated around were dozens of
as they listened to how

of how evil happened. Sometimes, hours would pass. One day, as I was feeling powerless to depart, two things dawned on me: The first was recognition of my boundless curiosity about criminality; the second was that I was not alone. Seated all around me in the gallery were dozens of other people, gap-jawed and silent as they listened to the story of how the defendant had gone wrong. For me, that day, that moment in court, was a literary "Eureka." I felt that as an author I'd finally found a subject I was passionate about—and that a lot of other people would care about too.

While not everyone wants to go as far as I have—thinking about crime, plots and evidence for most of one's waking hours—this book is a testimonial to the riveting effect crime has on most of us. Quick:

sace seizes our attention because it carries a simple message: Crime is unpredictable; no one is entirely safe. Not even wealth, fame and style can insulate us from the hand of evil. Ironically, the murders of people living everyday lives carry much the same message: No one is exempt.

Which is why the second phase—catching the perp—fascinates us as well. We want to believe that evil doesn't occur unchecked. Generally, the best crime stories propel us not only with an intense interest in the original, horrifying events, but also with a resulting desire to see the perpetrators apprehended and punished. We live out a familiar fable with a time-tested moral: Crime does not pay. We need to see the bad guy get it.

That's not all, of course. In my years in court, I have

been repeatedly struck by how many of us who make our livings on the sidelines of crime—cops and prosecutors, judges and defense lawyers and court personnel—have an uneasy fascination with the sordid high jinks of the folks who get themselves in trouble. Part of that, I'd argue, is because there can be as much, or more, imagination displayed in the universe of crime than in the world of art. What novelist could even conceive of a blind bank robber like Robert Toye—successful in 17 attempts before cops finally took him, and his cane, into custody—whose story is recounted in these pages?

So I've come to accept that among those who choose to deal with crime on a daily basis there is an ele-

or restaurant knowing they'd received too much in change? Or never hooked up a splitter to their cable line? At the same time, reporters will tell you that some crimes just don't make good copy—the sexual exploitation of children is the best example—and that I think is because those are desires that most of us find simply intolerable.

By contrast, many of the crimes in this book have intrigued us, I think, because they touch on the darker fantasies of many of us. The good news: The law doesn't punish us merely for thinking badly. As Justice Holmes remarked long ago, crimes require the combination of the evil-thinking mind *with* the evil-doing hand.

people, gap-jawed and silent the defendant had gone wrong'

ment of attraction too. Occasionally these affinities become overt. Cops go wrong all the time. So do lawyers, like Thomas Capano, a former Delaware deputy attorney general, who murdered his mistress and sank her body in the Atlantic. His story, too, is described here. But generally speaking, most law-enforcement professionals manage to satisfy their curiosity without damage to themselves or anybody else. For cops and lawyers, the satisfying denouement comes when the bad guy goes to jail and we go home. Still, we often leave the courthouse knowing that the impulse the criminal could not subdue is one we have sometimes felt ourselves. For me it is an article of faith that all of us occasionally experience an inclination to violence and dishonesty. How many people can say that they never walked out of a store

In the end, I think our core curiosity about crime is learning why people surrender to their dark impulses. We want to answer that question, not simply as lurid voyeurs but in order to learn the warning signals before we ourselves stray over the line. Ultimately, crime stories reinforce our moral fiber by showing us why we want to keep a firm hold on our ugliest desires, and they respond to our eternal curiosity about how and why people go wrong. We all live close enough to the edge that we need to understand.

Writer and attorney **Scott Turow** is the author of six bestselling novels, including *Presumed Innocent* and *The Burden of Proof.* A partner in the Chicago office of Sonnenschein Nath & Rosenthal, he specializes in white-collar criminal defense.

A radiant Laci Peterson could scarcely contain her joy on her wedding day in 1997.

"I can only hope that the sound of Laci's voice begging for her life, begging for the life of her unborn child, is heard over and over again in the mind of [their killer] every day for the rest of his life."

LACI'S MOM, SHARON ROCHA

IN COLD BLOOD

In the catalogue of personal evils, it is perhaps the most heinous crime: first-degree murder. It's simple, and chilling. One person decides to kill another person. Not to wish that person away, not to daydream in anger, but to become the conscious, active agent in someone else's death. They plot, they plan. They assemble what they need—a gun, a boat, a bag of cement, an alibi. They know or learn their intended victim's habits, pick a day and time, and then commit murder—sudden, hands-on and very personal.

Often—and almost always in cases that make headlines for weeks on end—the killer seems guy-next-door normal until the day he (or she, though women make up only 7 percent of murderers) acts. They hold jobs, play golf, treat pets nicely, smile in family photos. No one saw it coming.

And that, in all likelihood, lies at the heart of our fascination. Until that moment, they often seem…just like us.

HOW COULD HE DO IT?

They were the couple on the wedding cake, five years later: cute, living in the burbs, expecting their first child. Then Laci Peterson vanished— and cops uncovered her smooth-talking husband's secret life

AS SCOTT PETERSON LATER TOLD POLICE, HE HAD returned home around 5 p.m. on Christmas Eve, 2002, from a fishing trip to discover his wife Laci's Land Rover parked in the driveway, her purse in the house and no sign of anyone. His initial response? He took a shower. Only then did Peterson, 30, begin to make frantic phone calls to friends and family, looking for Laci, 27, who was eight months pregnant. "He was panicked and very emotional," Laci's sister Amy Rocha recalled. "He just said, 'Is your sister with you?'"

Over the next two years, of course, Laci's disappearance became much more than a missing persons mystery. The case had no celebrities, no cameras in the courtroom and relatively little hard evidence, but it kept Americans mesmerized. Ultimately the saga of Scott and Laci offered a chilling glimpse of the dark side of the American Dream: the attractive young

Friends and family had no inkling of any real domestic troubles between Laci and Scott.

expectant parents, the tidy house in the suburbs, the boundless promise that seemed theirs—and the charming husband who turned out to be a ruthless killer. "There's too much love there," said Laci's stepfather Ron Grantski, explaining in the days after Laci went missing why no one in the family could believe that Scott had anything to do with it.

From the outset, though, investi-

In a 2003 interview with Diane Sawyer Peterson lied, saying he had told cops about cheating on Laci.

MISSING
$500,000 REWARD
For information leading to her safe return

Laci (Rocha) Peterson

Age: 27   Height: 5'1"
Eyes: Brown   Hair: Brown
8 Months Pregnant

Call MODESTO P.D. at **209-342-6166**
or visit
lacipeterson.com

Laci was last seen 12/24/02 at 9:30am. She was believed to be heading toward Dry Creek in Modesto, CA to walk her golden retriever. She was wearing a white long sleeve shirt and black pants. Laci also has a sunflower tattoo on her left ankle.

Shortly after Laci went missing, Peterson said he was going to put up posters, but he was spotted dropping by the golf course instead.

gators had privately pegged Scott as their most likely suspect. For starters, when police questioned him about his fishing expedition to San Francisco Bay on the day Laci disappeared, he couldn't tell them what kind of bait he had used. It also emerged that the last time anyone other than Scott could say they had seen or heard from Laci was the evening of Dec. 23, when she talked on the phone with her mother, Sharon Rocha. His behavior raised even more questions in the weeks that followed. At a candlelight vigil for Laci just days after she vanished, Scott was spotted grinning and chatting as if he hadn't a care in the world.

That sort of thing only dented his credibility; the bombshell came on Jan. 24 when Amber Frey, now 30, a massage therapist from Fresno, stepped before a bank of microphones and announced that she and Scott had been having an affair. They had met on a blind date in November 2002, and Scott, she said, had assured her that he was single. Within a few weeks, he had quietly bought the boat that he would use for his Christmas Eve fishing trip and had scanned the Internet for tide patterns in San Francisco Bay—actions

While Peterson enjoyed himself with Amber Frey at a holiday party in 2002, Laci was home alone.

THE TELL-TALE TAPES

Peterson's first lawyer warned him against baring his soul to lover Amber Frey.

Amber Frey went to police shortly after discovering that Scott Peterson was not only married but that his wife had disappeared. The authorities urged her to continue the relationship and to secretly tape her conversations with Peterson in the hope that he would confess or otherwise incriminate himself. Frey recorded hundreds of calls, many of which, like these excerpts, were played in court.

JAN. 6, 2003
Scott: I lied to you that I've been traveling. . . . The girl I'm married to, her name is Laci. . . . She disappeared before Christmas.
Amber: You came to me in early December and told me you lost your wife. What was that about?
Scott: She's alive. . . . The media has been telling everyone that I had something to do with her disappearance. . . . I hope so much that this doesn't hurt you. . . . You deserve so much better.
Amber: Yeah, and I deserve . . . an explanation of why you told

me you lost your wife and this was the first holidays you'd spend without her. . . . You sat there in front of me and cried and broke down. I sat there and held your hand, Scott, and comforted you, and you have lied to me.
Scott: Yeah.
Amber: Didn't you say, "Amber, I will do anything for you to trust me. . . . I feel we have a future together."
Scott: I never said anything to you that I didn't mean.
JAN. 7
Amber: Scott, you really haven't done everything you can yet [to find Laci]. You

don't speak in public. . . . You have nothing to hide?
Scott: No. . . . Everyone's the suspect.
Amber: And you haven't [gone] before the media . . . to plead innocent of any of this?
Scott: I am innocent. I don't have to plead it.
Amber: [I have a] fear inside my heart that you had something to do with this and that you may have . . . killed your wife.
Scott: No, you don't need to have that fear. I lied to you. But I'm not an evil person.
JAN. 8
Amber: So, did you love Laci and your baby?
Scott: I love Laci. I loved Laci, no question.
Amber: So you loved her, but there's me. How does that make sense? How . . . can I make sense of that?

that prosecutors later said showed he was already hatching a plot to dump his wife's body. When Frey found out in early December that Peterson was in fact married, he lied again, telling her that he had "lost" his wife and that this would be his first Christmas without her. Frey accepted his explanation. "It was my job to be there for him," she later wrote, "and to be as understanding as humanly possible."

For those who had been following the case, reaction to the news of Peterson's relationship with Frey was considerably more skeptical. Surveys early in 2003 showed that nearly 80 percent of those polled believed he was guilty. Then came the harshest discoveries of all: In April the bodies of Laci and the baby the couple had planned to name Conner washed up on the shores of San Francisco Bay. As a deputy district attorney in L.A. county drily put it, "What a coincidence that of all the places in California or the western United States the body just happens to wash ashore in the place where he went fishing."

Attorney Mark Geragos (center) got off to a strong start but ultimately put forward a surprisingly skimpy defense for his client.

Within days police arrested Peterson near the Mexican border. He had dyed his hair orange, stuffed his car with camping gear and was carrying $15,000 in cash—all of which left the distinct impression that he had been nabbed on the brink of making a break for freedom.

At the opening of the trial in June 2004, Peterson's lawyer Mark Geragos boldly assured the jury he would prove his client was "stone-cold innocent." It did not work out that way. Though prosecutors sometimes went into eye-glazing detail, they managed to present a devastating circumstantial case against Peterson. Among the highlights was their demonstration that only 10 minutes could have elapsed between the time Peterson left the house on the morning of Dec. 24—when he said he last saw Laci, who was heading out to walk the dog—and the time that a neighbor found the dog wandering loose.

Once again the star witness was Amber Frey, who had started taping her calls with Scott shortly after hearing news reports about Laci's disappearance. On the tapes, among other things, Scott could be heard pretending to be in Europe over the New Year's holiday—he gave her a moving description of fireworks over the Eiffel Tower—while in reality he was in Modesto, supposedly looking for his lost wife.

WHAT HAPPENED: After a five-month trial but only 7½ hours of deliberations, the jury found Peterson guilty of first-degree murder. A month later, on Dec. 13, the same panel voted in favor of the death penalty. On March 16 Judge Alfred Delucchi formally sentenced Peterson to death. The next day he was transferred in shackles and leg irons to San Quentin's death row; it is very unlikely, though, that he will face execution anytime soon, given that it can take five years or more for an appeal to be heard. Throughout the trial Peterson showed little emotion beyond a wintry smirk. Ultimately there was no penetrating his facade or figuring out the motive that drove him to murder. As Laci's mother, Sharon, screamed at Peterson during her testimony in the sentencing phase of the trial, "Divorce is always an option, not murder!" Scott Peterson sat impassively, seemingly untouched to the end.

Laci's body (left), recovered in San Francisco Bay in April 2003, was badly decomposed; by contrast, Conner's was well preserved.

In her diary, Fahey (below)
wrote that she was
tired of her "manipulative"
lover, Capano.

LOVER, LAWYER—
AND KILLER

T WAS ALL A TRAGIC ACCIDENT, THOMAS Capano told a jury. The former chief counsel to the governor of Delaware, Capano, 49, had taken Anne Marie Fahey, 30, his mistress and the governor's scheduling secretary, to dinner and afterward brought her to his home. That same evening, June 27, 1996, he claimed, another woman arrived, accused him of using her and brandished a gun in a jealous rage. She and Capano struggled, the weapon went off, and Fahey fell to the floor. The woman fled and, in a panic, Capano stuffed Fahey's body into an ice cooler, then cruised out into the Atlantic and tried to sink her. When he could not sink the cooler, he chained Fahey's body to a couple of anchors and shoved her overboard. The jury didn't buy it, perhaps finding Fahey's diary more persuasive. Writing that Capano, now on death row, was a "jealous maniac," she was ready to dump him. When Capano found out, he resolved not to let that happen.

Teen Love,
Teen Murder

EVERYONE WHO KNEW THEM agreed: Diane Zamora and David Graham, both 18, were virtuous, ambitious and deeply in love. Zamora had landed a coveted appointment to the Naval Academy in Annapolis and dreamed of exploring space. Graham had enrolled in the Air Force Academy and hoped to become a fighter pilot. Emotionally inseparable since they began dating in high school in Mansfield, Texas, they planned to marry as soon as they graduated from military school.

That won't be happening.

For nine months in 1996, police in Grand Prairie, Texas, had puzzled over a brutal slaying. Adrianne Jones, 16, a Mansfield student and an athletic beauty, had been found dead in a remote area outside of town, her skull cracked and her face mutilated by gunshot wounds. Police had no suspects, no leads and little hope. They also had no idea they were about to get their big break.

That August, newly arrived naval cadet Zamora sat with a couple of confidantes and regaled them with stories about her beloved Graham and the magical future they would share. Then, well into their little bull session, she revealed a darker secret: Back in high school she had been involved in a killing. Graham claimed that in a moment of weakness he had slept with a girl named Jones. Zamora had flown into a rage, screaming, "Kill her, kill her!"

Shortly afterward, they lured Jones out of town for what they promised would be a quiet talk. Instead, Zamora clubbed the girl with a barbell, and Graham killed her with two shots from a 9-mm handgun. Zamora said she felt bad, but she and Graham went to church to find solace. "I know God has

Zamora (right) and Graham were all smiles as they prepared to go off to their respective military schools.

forgiven us," she later said.

Zamora's fellow cadets, silently horrified, immediately went to superiors. "She said anyone who got between her and David would have to die," one cadet recalled. "She said . . . the girl deserved it . . . everyone knew the girl was a tramp."

After Zamora's trial in the winter of

The victim, Adrianne Jones (right), was on the cross-country team with Graham.

1998, Linda Jones, the victim's mother, lamented that her late daughter would have graduated soon. Instead of mourning Adrianne, she added, "she and I should be looking for prom dresses."

THE VERDICT: Found guilty in separate trials, Zamora and Graham were convicted of capital murder and sentenced to life in prison with the possibility of parole after 40 years.

THE RIDDLE OF VERSACE'S KILLER

Versace's South Beach home was just one of his palatial estates.

PAYING FOR A HANDFUL OF magazines at a Miami Beach cafe the morning of July 15, 1997, designer Gianni Versace strolled home to Casa Casuarina, the Mediterranean-style palazzo where he regularly entertained the likes of Madonna and Sly Stallone. As he reached his front gate, a young man in a white shirt, gray shorts and a black backpack walked up, drew a gun and shot Versace twice in the head. The young man, reported one witness, "continued on his way down the street as if nothing had happened."

Swarming through the neighborhood, police didn't find the perp but, three blocks away, they discovered a 1995 red pickup that had been stolen from another murder victim, William Reese, a cemetery caretaker who had been shot to death in southern New Jersey. Reese was one of four men presumed slain by the same unlikely suspect: Andrew Cunanan, a handsome 27-year-old who had enjoyed a pampered existence growing up in San Diego.

Instead of taking advantage of his obvious intelligence—Cunanan had reportedly read an entire set of encyclopedias by age 14—the young Californian became a high-priced gigolo who preyed on older men. Apparently, he embarked on his month-long killing spree—which earned him a spot on the FBI's Most Wanted list—after gaining weight and losing some

Cunanan mentioned Versace's name to friends as if they had once met.

of the allure necessary to his chosen profession. As the chase went on Cunanan, who proved adept at disguise, repeatedly changed his look.

Two days after Versace's death, the owner of a sailboat in a marina near the designer's home phoned police to say that he had seen a man resembling Cunanan. By the time police arrived, the man had slipped away. Then, on the afternoon of July 23, Fernando Carreira, who watched over boats for wealthy owners, dropped by to check on a two-story houseboat owned by a German businessman. Seeing a light on inside, Carreira drew his gun. Before he could make a move, a shot rang out, and Carreira fled to call police.

Just after 8 p.m., a SWAT team swarmed the boat, only to find Cunanan upstairs, dead from a gunshot wound to the head. No one ever learned why Cunanan had targeted Versace, but some observers suggested that in killing such a famous man, Cunanan finally achieved a measure of the celebrity status he coveted.

THE SMOKING GUN: The pistol found in Cunanan's lap—a key piece of evidence—turned out to be the same gun that had killed Versace.

Charles claimed a robber had left him and his wife, Carol, for dead on this deserted street.

A Dark Night for the City of Boston

AFTER THEIR BIRTHING CLASS BROKE UP, CHARLES STUART AND his wife, Carol, an attorney who was seven months pregnant, made their way to their car in the parking lot of Boston's Brigham and Women's Hospital. They planned to hurry through the hospital's crime-plagued neighborhood and make their way to their comfortable home in the suburb of Reading. But pulling up to a red light two blocks away, Charles, 30, later claimed, they were confronted by an African-American man brandishing a .38. He forced his way into the car and ordered the couple to drive to an isolated street. There he accused Charles of being a cop, jammed the gun into the back of Carol's head and pulled the trigger. He then shot Charles in the abdomen, snatched some cash and jewelry and fled.

Stuart survived, but locals were enraged by the cold-blooded execution of a pregnant woman and demanded retribution. The city was on the verge of a racially divided meltdown when, 10 weeks later, on Jan. 3, 1990, Charles's younger brother Matthew arrived at police headquarters. The night Carol, 30, was shot, Matthew told them, he and a friend met Charles on a dark street, where he gave them a gun and Carol's purse, which they then dumped in the river. Matthew could no longer hold his secrets—and Charles apparently sensed that something was up. Early the next day he parked his car on Boston's Tobin Bridge, left a note reading, "The allegations have taken all my strength," and leaped to his death in the murky Mystic River.

Charles and Carol seemed eager for their first child.

THE MOTIVE: Some thought Charles wanted insurance money so he could open a restaurant. But no one is really certain what drove him to kill.

"From the first second, he worshipped her," a friend recalled of Mark Hacking (with Lori).

A TAPESTRY OF LIES

Mark Hacking seemed to be a doting husband bound for medical school. Then his wife, Lori, vanished—and his life of lies unraveled

LORI HACKING WAS THE first to concede that her husband, Mark, was the more romantic of the two. Sparks first flew for the Salt Lake City natives during a high school outing at Lake Powell. He proved to be a doting suitor. "He'd set a candlelight dinner with a long-stemmed rose across her plate," recalled Lori's mother, Thelma Soares. They both enrolled at the University of Utah and were married in 1999, shortly after she received her business degree.

Taking a job at a local Wells Fargo bank branch, Lori got her career off to a fast start, impressing bosses and colleagues alike as a promising sales assistant in the brokerage department. Still working on his undergraduate degree, Mark gladly gave Lori all the support he could, making most of the meals and keeping the house in order. Not one to squander his time, he also signed on as an aide at local University Neuropsychiatric Institute, helping patients settle in.

In May of 2004, after years of hard work, Mark proudly sent out invitations for his graduation day—though he fell suddenly sick and missed his own commencement. That disappointment quickly melted away when he got word that he had been accepted to medical school at George Washington University in Washington, D.C. That news was trumped just days later, when he heard he had been bumped up on the waiting list for the higher-ranked University of North Carolina. "He talked about costs of the college, national rankings, loans he would need," said a friend. He was so excited he rushed out and bought himself a shiny new stethoscope.

Lori, 27, and Mark, 28, seemed destined for success. Then, on July 16, 2004, a coworker overheard Lori talking on the phone. "But he's already been accepted," Lori said into the receiver. "He's already applied. This can't be correct." After hanging up, she broke down in sobs and had to leave work.

Still, at a party two nights later, Lori appeared jubilant, celebrating the fact that she and Mark were moving to Chapel Hill, N.C. Better yet, she had just learned that she was five weeks pregnant with their first child.

The next day, Mark, sounding desperate, phoned Lori's office to say that she had gone for a jog in nearby Memory Grove Park, a hangout for transients, and had never come back. Concerned coworkers raced to the park to search for her. Instead of joining them, Mark drove to a mattress store

'They took pictures of him in his cap and gown. He had thought everything out' —LORI'S BROTHER PAUL SOARES

After searching for 10 weeks, law-enforcement officers found Lori's body in a local landfill.

MISSING
FROM CITY CREEK CANYON OR MEMORY GROVE AREA

LORI HACKING
27 YEARS OLD 5'4" 100 LBS
**PLEASE CONTACT POLICE: 799-3000
WITH ANY INFORMATION**

Mark told police Lori had gone for a morning jog and had never returned.

where credit card records showed he purchased a new mattress at 10:23 a.m. Nearly a half hour later, at 10:49, he notified police his wife was missing. Only then did he head for the park.

The following night, a security guard at a local hotel summoned police to remove a naked man who was wandering around the parking lot. The wanderer was Mark Hacking, so clearly disoriented that the police hauled him off to a psychiatric unit. It was time, police decided, to take a closer look at the grieving husband.

It didn't take them long to discover that Hacking had never been accepted to medical school. In fact, he had never graduated from college. Then police found bloodstains on the headboard and sideboard of the couple's bed, as well as strands of hair on a knife.

Visiting Mark in the psychiatric clinic on July 24, his two brothers pressed him for the truth. He had previously assured their father, a doctor as he had hoped to be, that he had had nothing to do with Lori's disappearance. This time, he came clean, saying, "Lori's dead and I killed her." He described how he and Lori had gotten into a fight after she found out he had lied about medical school. After she went to bed, he played video games, did a little bit of packing, then, as she slept, crept up to the bed and shot Lori in the head with a .22-cal. rifle. Wrapping her body in garbage bags, he drove to the University of Utah campus and dumped her body, the gun and part of the blood-stained mattress into three separate trash bins.

Desperate to find an explanation for his bizarre behavior, Mark's mother suggested that his personality had gone through a change after he fell off a roof in his 20s and hurt his head. Ever since, she insisted, "he has had a hard time concentrating."

While the search in the local park was called off, a new one began at the local dump, where law-enforcement personnel spent 10 hours a day, four days a week, combing through 4,600 tons of garbage before Lori's remains were discovered. "He's relieved and grateful they found her," Mark's brother Lance said. But judging by his subsequent actions in court, he was not entirely repentant.

On Oct. 29 Mark pleaded not guilty to first-degree murder—much to the horror of his and Lori's families, both of whom wanted desperately to avoid a trial. "Just tell the truth," urged Lori's brother Paul Soares in a letter. "... Have you ever told the truth?"

UPDATE: On April 15, 2005, Mark Hacking pleaded guilty to murder, saving the families the pain of a trial.

Pure Evil, Random Murder

THE THREE WOMEN HAD VANISHED. Visiting Yosemite National Park, Carole Sund, 42, a property manager from Eureka, Calif., her daughter Juli, 15, and Silvina Pelosso, 16, a friend from Argentina, had checked into the Cedar Lodge in nearby El Portal and, judging by the wet towels, spent the night, then showered before going out. After that . . . not a trace.

It wasn't until a month later, March 18, 1999, that police found Sund's car—84

Juli Sund (right) and family friend Silvina Pelosso paused to enjoy the wonders of Yosemite.

miles away in a clearing off a rural highway. It bore the dark scars of a raging fire, and in the trunk police found the charred remains of Sund and Pelosso. After an anonymous tip, police later discovered Juli's body at a scenic overlook; her throat had been cut. There was more: On July 22 authorities found the body of Joie Ruth Armstrong, 26, a popular local naturalist, who had been ruthlessly decapitated.

Cary Stayner, 37, the handyman at the lodge, was one of the first to be interviewed by the FBI, and he had been cleared. But shortly after Armstrong's body was discovered, a park employee reported seeing Stayner's SUV near Armstrong's cabin. Police tracked him down to a nudist camp near Sacramento, where he admitted he had slain Armstrong—for no good reason.

The other murders were not solved until the next day, when a TV news reporter reached Stayner for a jailhouse interview. In answer to a question about the first three killings, Stayner volunteered, "I did it—I'm guilty." He went on to explain how he had felt the urge to kill women since he was 7 years old. Sund and the girls had simply been in the wrong place at the wrong time.

He confessed that he strangled Sund and Pelosso in their room and stuffed their bodies in the car before snatching Juli from her room. He killed them all the night they arrived, dampening their towels to make it look as if they had spent the night. And it had been Stayner who tipped police off to where they would find Juli's body.

THE VERDICT: Found guilty of all four murders, Stayner waits on death row in San Quentin. He told a reporter that he would have kept killing women until he was finally caught.

For Stayner (in custody, below), the murders of Carole Sund (top) and Joie Ruth Armstrong (above) might just have been the beginning.

After his arrest, Richard Crafts (below, left) continued to insist that his wife, Helle (below, right), was alive. Police were convinced that she had met with a violent end and later determined that he had disposed of her body with a rented two-ton woodchipper.

A Shred of Evidence Solves a Grim Mystery

SHORTLY AFTER LANDING AT JFK INTERNATIONAL AIRPORT, HELLE Crafts and two fellow flight attendants loaded their bags into a car for the long drive home. It took an hour for them to reach her stop, Crafts's four-bedroom ranch house in rural Newtown, Conn. Seeing a light on, she chirped, "Oh, Richard's home," gathered her belongings and said goodbye.

The date was Nov. 18, 1986. A wicked storm blew in that night, blanketing the state with snow and pulling down power lines, leaving the Craftses' home dark and cold. At 6 a.m. Richard Crafts, 48, an Eastern Airlines pilot, roused the three children and their nanny and bundled them into the car to seek refuge at his sister's home in Westport, Conn., 30 miles away. Helle, he told them, had gone ahead. When they reached the house, they learned that Helle had never arrived. After breakfast, Richard returned to Newtown. Power was restored by mid-morning, but he didn't return for his children until that evening. Helle, Richard told everyone, had rushed back to her native Denmark to be with her sick mother.

A couple of days later, the nanny noticed a curious stain on the master-bedroom carpet, which Richard dismissed as a spill from a portable kerosene heater. Rather than clean the spot, he ripped up the carpet and took it to the dump.

Helle, 39, who had a flawless record with Pan Am, failed to arrive in time for her next flight, and her bosses and fellow employees were mystified. Richard

insisted she had flown to Denmark, but when they called Helle's mother, she said she was perfectly fit and had not seen her daughter. That was particularly troubling to friends with whom Helle had shared a foreboding secret: She had begun to believe her husband was having an affair, a suspicion that was verified when a private detective she hired presented her with a photograph taken of Richard kissing an Eastern Airlines flight attendant. Helle told friends that she had confronted her husband, and he had seemed strangely aloof. That worried her. "If something happens to me," she told friends, "please don't assume it was an accident."

Initially police ignored the case, convinced by Richard's story that Helle had left of her own free will. Their reluctance changed when Joe Hine, a highway worker, came forward with a curious story: He had been plowing snow off side roads shortly after Helle vanished and had come across a man standing beside an industrial-size woodchipper hitched to a U-Haul truck. Hine was baffled: Why in the world, he asked himself, would someone chip wood in the middle of a snowstorm?

Two detectives accompanied him to the remote site, where they found a pile of frozen wood chips. Among the detritus, they unearthed a torn envelope with Helle Crafts's name. Police were horrified by their inevitable conclusion. "It was just too much to believe someone could do something so inhuman," said one inspector. Using kerosene heaters to thaw the ground, police scoured the debris, finally recovering minute fragments of flesh, bone and, most telling of all, two teeth, which proved to be Helle's.

THE VERDICT: The total weight of the evidence was less than two ounces. But that was enough: Richard Crafts was convicted of capital murder and sentenced to 50 years.

"I was in love," testified Billy Flynn (left), explaining why he let Smart (far left) sweet talk him into murder.

gloves, pounced on him and forced him to his knees. Flynn drew a .38-cal. handgun that belonged to a friend's father, aimed it at Gregg's head and, after a moment's hesitation, pulled the trigger. When Pam arrived home later, her screams roused startled neighbors.

Police had a tough time cracking the case until a snitch told them he had heard the boys talking about the murder. Added to Smart's own confession, caught on tape by a student aide police had outfitted with a wire, the jury had little trouble convicting Smart of murder and sending her to jail for life.

TOO SMART? Smart wasn't worried, she told the student aide wearing the wire, because if it came down to her word versus the boys', she was a respected counselor and police "are going to believe me."

THE TEACHER'S PET GETS 28 YEARS

THIS WAS MORE THAN THE KIND of puppy love Billy Flynn was used to. Pam Smart, 22, an administrator at Winnacunnet High in Hampton, N.H., had invited the 15-year-old sophomore to her condo—while her husband was away. She pushed a copy of the steamy film *9½ Weeks* into the VCR and they sat back to enjoy. Afterward she re-created the striptease Kim Basinger performed in the movie. Then, as heavy metal blasted on the stereo, they had sex.

Before long, Smart began to confide in her young lover. She complained that her husband, Gregg, a 24-year-old insurance salesman, had become boring and abusive. She told Flynn they might split up, but she feared that scenario because Gregg would get everything they owned, including their Shih Tzu Halen, named after the rock star.

Couldn't Flynn help? she whimpered. There was no mistaking what she meant. She suggested that Flynn recruit three of his buddies, then stage a break-in one night when Smart was at a school board meeting. But, she

warned, don't kill Gregg in front of Halen, because it could traumatize the dog.

When Gregg arrived home around 9 p.m. on May 1, 1990, Flynn and a pal, both dressed in dark clothes and wearing latex

Less than a year after their wedding, Smart was plotting to have Gregg killed.

Toye used a miniature telescope to read the fine print in the Manhattan phone book and pick his targets.

"I've been in the business since I was 16. . . . I always wanted to rob banks. My idols were Al Capone and Jesse James."

ROBERT VERNON TOYE

THE UNUSUAL SUSPECTS

S ome crimes are intriguing because of their dark drama, their unsettling echo of atavistic urges, our ambivalent fascination with violence, or what they say about our society, our nation, our world.

These aren't those crimes. The cases in this chapter stand out, for the most part, because they're . . . odd. They're crimes that make you go "Hmmm . . ." Or, more precisely, *"Wha????"* Why would a blind man become a bank robber? (More curiously: How did he succeed?) Who marries 82 times? Or commits 3,300 burglaries? Why would a successful doctor claim to have access to a sperm bank when he was really the sole supplier?

Enough questions. Better they explain it themselves.

WANTED

40638

FOR ARMED BANK ROBBERY

The above photographs depict one ROBERT VERNON TOYE, a white male, 34 years (11/25/48), 5'9", 180 lbs., brown hair, possible mustache, beard or combination of both. Subject suffers from Retinitis Pigmentosa (Night Blindness), and has diminished peripheral vision. Subject wears plain metal or black rimmed eyeglasses. Subject has numerous tattoos on his arms, chest and body. Subject seeks the company of transexuals.

Subject is armed with a handgun, and is suicidal/homicidal. APPROACH WITH EXTREME CAUTION.

Any information concerning the whereabouts of this individual should be transmitted to the Joint Bank Robbery Task Force, at 553-2816 during business hours, and 553-2700 at other times. Special Agent Henry Garcia and Detective Tom Nerney assigned.

| CIRCULAR NO.83/114 DATE PREPARED 5/13/83 | **POLICE DEPARTMENT** CITY OF NEW YORK | LIMITED TO DEPARTMENT CIRCULATION |

Toye had become such a nuisance that police issued posters in New York City. He was nabbed shortly afterward.

THE TALE OF THE BLIND BANK ROBBER

Robert Vernon Toye was legally blind, but that didn't stop the enterprising heistmeister from knocking over 17 banks

ROWING UP IN SAN PEDRO, CALIF., ROBERT VERNON TOYE set his sights on what seemed like a daring career: robbing banks. It wouldn't be easy, for more than the obvious reasons. Toye suffers from retinitis pigmentosa, an incurable degenerative eye disease. When he pulled his first heist, in 1974, he could barely see. He had just been released from prison, where he had served time for more pedestrian crimes. "I told the cabdriver I had to go by the bank to pick up some money," he later recalled. He did—$8,000 that he instructed a teller to stuff into a brown paper bag.

It took some time for Toye to perfect his technique. With what little he could see out of his right eye, he would focus on the back of someone's shoe and follow that person to the teller's window. "Young people walk too fast, so I'd wait

'If I get in a money bind and need a few thousand fast, I know where to find it'

for an old person," he recalled. At the window he passed the teller a note with his signature card—a one-eyed Jack on which he had written, "Be quick, be quiet or you're dead. Put all the cash in the bag. I have a gun." (He never actually carried a gun.) Afterward he tapped his way toward the door, where a courteous guard, seeing the white cane, would show him out.

In all, Toye knocked off 17 banks, hauling in as much as $18,000 in a single score. In the 1980s business was so brisk that he lived a dual life, whooping it up in Vegas until his loot was low, then flying back to New York to rebuild his stake with another bank job. In his own way, Toye was a great success, though he did on occasion get a bit overconfident. Once, in the middle of a job, a woman cut in line in front of him at the teller's window. "Dammit, lady," he growled, "I'm robbing this bank."

Toye was nabbed in 1983, when he was spotted by a task force on the lookout for a blind bank robber who favored Citibank branches. Uncowed in prison after a conviction for nine counts of bank robbery, he made a break for it, using his cane to help him climb over two perimeter fences. Outside the compound, he took off at a dead run. Which worked just fine until he smacked into a pine tree— and guards picked him up.

HINDSIGHT: Toye had spent more than half his life behind bars, but expressed few regrets. He even did some good with his ill-gotten gains, donating $35,000 to a research group trying to find a cure for retinitis pigmentosa.

The Seer Who Didn't See It Coming

Miss Cleo said she offered heartfelt advice and had no idea that her callers were being exploited.

TV CLAIRVOYANT MISS CLEO BECAME A PHENOM SHORTLY AFTER SHE first appeared in TV promos for Access Resource Services in Fort Lauderdale. In a lilting Caribbean accent, she advised callers on matters of love, money and just about anything else. The problem was that callers—despite ads touting free tarot-card sessions—were charged as much as $4.99 a minute.

Plus Cleo, 40, who claimed her first mystical experience came when a deceased uncle dropped by when she was 14, was really Youree Dell Harris, a preppy theater student from L.A. who had invented the Jamaican seer for a staged monologue. The TV show was canceled in 2002 and Miss Cleo was charged with deceptive trade practices. That accusation was dropped, but ARS did forgive a stunning $500 million in callers' debt. Miss Cleo, it seemed, never divined her own fall from grace.

The feds claimed some folks who never even called were charged.

Call Now for Free!

1-800-
First 3 minutes of each call FREE! Must be 18. For entertainment only.

THE ART OF THE SCAM

THE GOOD NEWS, FOR ARTIST John Myatt, was that his works were selling splendidly—up to $40,000 a pop at the finest auction houses for a single abstract still life. The bad news: The names signed to the works were, among others, Chagall, Giacometti and Dubuffet. "I thought, Everyone's got a guilty secret; this was mine," said the British master forger. He might have gotten away with it had his partner in crime, John Drewe, not dumped his girlfriend, who paid back the favor by going to the authorities and expos-

"I really thought I'd got away with it," says Myatt (with his Picasso-style self-portrait), who copied masters for eight years.

Just Say Neigh

NO WAY HE WAS DRUNK DRIVING, SAID WILLIS HAMMETT. FIRST of all, there was no car. Hammett, a 69-year-old cowpoke from Valley Springs, Calif., had set out down Highway 26 on his trusty steed, Jug, to quench his thirst at the local saloon. One drink led to another and, with Jug hitched to a flagpole outside, Hammett made a night of it. Then an officer from the Humane Society sashayed in and cast a stern look at Hammett. Leaving the animal tied up amounted to neglect, she warned, so he should ride Jug home, or she would take the horse to a shelter. What was said that night in December 1983 varies with who tells the tale, but everyone agreed that Hammett did some whooping and hollering on the highway with Jug, and as a consequence, the buckaroo spent the night in the pokey. He was first charged with drunk driving—according to state law then, anyone riding a horse on a highway was subject to the motor vehicle code. The charge was changed to drunk in public, but still Hammett demanded a trial—and was acquitted. "It was all a comedy of errors," one lawman said. When local folks heard what had happened, they hoped next time Jug would rein his master in.

ing the scam. The judge in Myatt's 1999 trial was firm but complimented him for cooperating with the investigation. The con artist ended up serving a mere four months in jail. When Myatt was released, he was stunned to find his brush with the law had made him something of a populist hero: People who had seen his works in court were so smitten that they began paying thousands for his phonies. In a hasty post-prison exhibition, he sold all but three of 68 "genuine fakes." A producer for a BBC documentary about Myatt bought a half dozen, and a detective who helped nab him later commissioned Myatt to paint his family portrait, saying, "He's got God-given talent. It would be nice for him to use it."

Hammett, (smooching Jug) says he sassed the officer a bit but meant no harm.

Jacobson maintained that he had not defrauded couples. They came to him for babies, he said, and he gave them babies.

CALL HIM THE SPERMINATOR

Dr. Cecil Jacobson told patients he had access to a sperm bank. In truth, he was the source—and may have fathered dozens of children

THE COUPLE TRIED FOR YEARS TO CONCEIVE, WITHOUT SUCCESS. Now they had hope. Dr. Cecil Jacobson, a fertility specialist, had helped dozens of distraught couples realize their dream. Sitting down with Jacobson in his Vienna, Va., office, they explained their plight. The husband had a low sperm count and some doctors had suggested they look into using a sperm bank. But they insisted that if they were ever going to have a child, it would have to be their direct offspring. So far, science had offered no solution. Jacobson was undaunted. "If you want a kid," he promised, "you're going to have a kid."

They did—by using what Jacobson said was a specially treated sample of the husband's semen. Artificially inseminated, the woman became pregnant and later gave birth to twins. The couple—like many of Jacobson's patients—were ecstatic.

But not for long. In the winter of 1992, the same couple, whose identity remained hidden throughout the ensuing legal wranglings, was horrified to learn Jacobson, 55, had been indicted on more than 50 counts of fraud and deception. A hulking, not terribly attractive man who soon earned the nick-

name the Sperminator, Jacobson was described by the prosecutor as either an egomaniac or heartless animal who perpetrated hideous scams on couples hoping to have children.

Scam One: Jacobson would inject women with a hormone he claimed would increase fertility. It was the same hormone that pregnancy kits test for. When home kits tested positive, Jacobson congratulated the women and suggested they start buying baby clothes. When they gained no weight and suffered no morning sickness, they began to worry. Jacobson tested them again and, afterward,

with condolences, said the fetuses were dead and would be "reabsorbed" into their bodies.

Scam Two was even more insidious. Prosecutors said Jacobson told patients he had access to a sperm bank and could supply a variety of traits, from hair color to high IQs. Employees and other witnesses later testified that they had never seen a storage facility or donors, and that prior to insemination procedures, Jacobson tended to disappear for long periods of time into the bathroom. Jacobson had no sperm bank of his own and had no agreement with any existing sperm bank; the semen he provided was his own. By the government's most alarming estimate, he had fathered more than 70 children by his patients.

Jacobson claimed to be mystified by the outcry. In fact, he added, his sperm might have even been safer than what he might have gotten from a sperm bank. "I knew my semen was safe," he said, "because I haven't slept with anyone but my wife in our 30 years of marriage."

Jacobson's wife, Joyce, was one of many defenders who argued that the case made no sense because the women wanted babies and they got babies. Besides, she added, "The sperm doesn't make the father. Anyone who got his sperm is lucky."

The jury begged to differ, finding Jacobson guilty on 52 counts of fraud and perjury. Jacobson lost his medical license, was sentenced to five years in prison and settled several medical malpractice suits.

THE TROUBLING LEGACY: Jacobson's punishment was little consolation for parents who grappled with the fact that six dozen children of roughly the same age were enrolled in Northern Virginia schools. What would happen, people asked, if they met—or worse, dated? One expert witness said, "If I was the parent of one of those children I would move away."

After Welch's arrest, more than 4,000 burglary victims lined up hoping to find their stolen property.

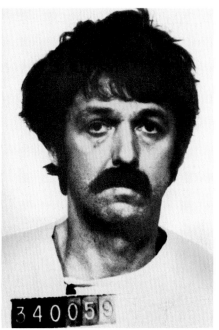

After 3,000 Burglaries: Time's Up

WHEN DR. MICHAEL HALBERSTAM, brother of author David Halberstam, returned to his Washington, D.C., home, he startled an intruder, who panicked and shot him. Halberstam, 48, died that night but police caught the perp. No ordinary burglar, the suspect turned out to be Bernard C. Welch Jr., 40, a.k.a. the Standard Time Burglar—so nicknamed because he preferred working in winter, when nights were long. Wanted for questioning in an astounding 3,300 burglaries and suspected of raping three women at gunpoint, Welch had recast himself as Norm Hamilton, a model citizen and collectibles dealer in Great Falls, Va., in the D.C. suburbs. Police needed six days to catalogue the 13,000 bits of booty, worth about $7 million, in his basement. They also found two smelters for melting down gold and silver. For his crimes, he was sentenced in 1981 to nine consecutive life terms. Welch proved to be a slippery character. Having broken out of prison once before, he did it again in 1985. Recaptured, this time he stayed put.

After months of tracking, Clark took satisfaction in Vigliotto's arrest: "My motto is, 'Do whatever you want to me, but the payback's a bitch.'"

GIOVANNI THE BIG-TIME BIGAMIST

WHEN SHARON CLARK, 41, ARRIVED AT THE PRE-arranged meeting place in Ontario, Canada, her husband, Giovanni Vigliotto, was nowhere to be found. Then it struck her: First he had sweet-talked her into marriage, then he loaded all the antiques from her flea-market business into a van and drove off. "I realized then," she says, "that he was rotten." She went after him, tracking Vigliotto from state to state for three months until she found him on Dec. 27, 1981, in a Panama City, Fla., shopping center. Vigliotto, police later confirmed, had scores of aliases and had married at least 82 times (he claimed 105). For his wandering ways, he was convicted of bigamy and fraud and sentenced to 34 years. "He spent lots of money on me," said Clark, recalling their more tender moments. Unfortunately, she adds, "it was probably all my own."

A Chorus of Voices, Just One Alleged Victim

RE-CREATING THAT AFTERNOON IN 1990, SARAH, 27, TOLD THE JURY THAT SHE had bumped into Mark Peterson simply by chance. She recognized the 29-year-old grocery clerk, the two talked for a bit, and they agreed to go to a local cafe. Afterward Peterson met Jennifer, a naive 20-year-old who loved to dance, and he left Sarah behind. Replacing Sarah on the witness stand, Jennifer recalled in a peculiar high-pitched voice that Peterson drove her to a park and "poked a hole in me with this thing."

The jury sat entranced. In all, they heard testimony from five women: Sarah, Jennifer, 6-year-old Emily, a matron named Franny, and Leslie, who said she found semen in Jennifer's shorts. Each witness was sworn in separately, each had a different voice—and each was Sarah, an Oshkosh, Wis., woman who suffered from multiple personality disorder.

Born in South Korea, Sarah—whose full name was never revealed because of the nature of the case—was orphaned at 8 months, then adopted by an Iowa City couple. She began hearing voices when she was 4 and later developed at least 46 different personalities. During the trial she summoned one personality, then another to address various aspects of the case. Initially Peterson was convicted, but the verdict was overturned. And that's where it ended: Fearing that a retrial might be psychologically harmful to Sarah, the district attorney chose not to retry the case.

"Franny," one of Sarah's 46 personalities, regretted introducing "Jennifer" to the clerk who was later accused of assaulting her. "I trusted that man, and he did harm to the body," testified Franny. "Sarah started to shake when we told her."

A Famous Oak Almost Croaks

LEGEND HAS IT THAT STEPHEN F. AUSTIN, founder of the Texas state capital, was standing under a massive oak when he signed a deal with the local Indians to acquire the land. The stately specimen was subsequently dubbed Treaty Oak, and Austin residents had revered the 600-year-old tree ever since. But in the summer of 1989, Texans learned that things were far from okay with the mighty oak: Leaves were falling. Branches were dying. An arborist made a quick, and disturbing, diagnosis: Poison! Indeed, the ground around the trunk had been soaked with a potent herbicide.

Residents filed by in a kind of deathbed vigil, leaving flowers, notes and even a can of chicken soup, as workers replaced the soil and dosed the tree with antitoxins. Finally cops caught the culprit, Paul Stedman Cullen, 45, a drifter who was subsequently sentenced to nine years for poisoning. "It had something to do with a girl he was trying to get over," said one confused officer. More important, the venerable oak survived—and Austin's roots were saved.

Dr. Bean-Bayog claimed Lozano "may have been an untreatable patient."

One overripe rumor: The tree was being sacrificed as part of a Satanic ritual.

IN THE FINAL ANALYSIS

WHEN TRADITIONAL PSYCHIATRIC METHods failed to help medical student Paul Lozano overcome depression, Harvard University's Dr. Margaret Bean-Bayog, 48, said, she tried a "regressive" therapy in which she played his mother. But on April 1, 1991, after four years of treatment, Lozano, 28, took his life with a lethal dose of cocaine. In his apartment police found erotic notes penned by Bean-Bayog. She claimed they were meant to help her privately exorcise her inappropriate feelings for Lozano and that he had stolen them from her office. Bean-Bayog was never charged with any crime and voluntarily surrendered her medical license. Lozano's family filed a wrongful-death suit against Bean-Bayog, claiming she had seduced their son and reduced him to a childlike state of dependency, then dropped him when his coverage ran out. "She psychologically and emotionally destroyed my brother," said his brother. The case was settled for $1 million.

Toto, with Frances before her trial, boasted he'd survived two gunshots.

LOVE HURTS

The rigged car didn't get him. Or the bullets. Or the baseball bat. And even though his wife tried to kill him, Tony Toto wanted her back

TONY TOTO NEVER SAW IT coming. As he stepped out of his front door in August 1982, he nearly tripped over a wire that had been rigged across the top of the steps. Unfazed, the 36-year-old Allentown, Pa., pizzeria owner couldn't imagine who had put it out there, and got on with his life. Days later a stranger came after him with a baseball bat. Luckily, the bat became tangled in a bush, and Toto escaped unscathed. But Toto began to wonder: Is someone out to get me?

Alas, yes. A few weeks later, Toto climbed into his 1982 Lincoln and tried the key. Nothing happened—which was the good news. Turned out that a wire had been stretched from the car's distributor cap to a spark plug that had been submerged in the gas tank (but didn't ignite). At this point Toto was almost certain something was not right.

It got worse. In January 1983 Toto was sound asleep when Anthony Bruno, 21, his daughter's boyfriend, crept into his bedroom, drew a pistol and shot Toto in the head. The bullet lodged in Toto's brain; he went into shock but didn't die. His loving wife, Frances, 38 at the time, nursed him back to health, feeding him chicken soup laced with Nytol—"To make sure that if I died, I would die in my sleep," Tony later explained.

The drama didn't end. Toto was again asleep when two teenagers snuck into his room and, with Tony's own gun, shot him in the heart. Or thought they did; the bullet actually passed through him, missing vital organs, and the redoubtable Toto got up to find out what the noise was all about.

The next night, the teenagers—cousins Ronald and Donald Barlip—bragged to a friend that they had been hired as hit men. The friend went to the cops, who rushed over to Tony's house. A police captain checked Tony out and, sure enough, he had a bullet wound in his chest. The captain then tried to question Toto's wife—only to learn that she had already called a lawyer. That was just as well: The officer arrested her on the spot for attempted murder.

Amazingly, as soon as Toto was strong enough, he came to his bride's defense, posting her bail, paying her lawyer and testifying on her behalf, blaming Bruno. "He sees I've got a nice home, a nice business, a nice family," said Toto, "and he's going to get it all."

Police didn't buy that, but after a little checking, they learned Toto liked the ladies, so maybe this was one of those "woman-scorned" cases. Still, Toto lamented his wife's conviction, saying, "According to the law, she's wrong, and I have to go along with the law. But in my heart, I know Frances is innocent." He even thought of opening a pizzeria near the jailhouse so he could visit her more easily.

THE VERDICT: Frances served four years in prison before being released and rejoining her husband. "We've got a lot of good years ahead of us," he had predicted before she went in.

Police found nine racks of designer clothes in Judy Dick's home.

A Shopper, A Copper, A Mom Who Got Stung

LOTS OF AFFLUENT FAMILIES IN ROSEVILLE, MINN., HAD NICE THINGS, but Judy Dick allegedly had something special: Her own designated shoplifter. Police claimed Dick would place orders for jewelry, clothes or other baubles with one Gregory Thomas, who would then go on a cash-free shopping spree—and offer the items for sale at prices no legit outlet could beat. The Dick family (Judy, 56, her husband, Gerald, 58, a dentist, and two of their children, James, 32, and Stacy, 33) was home Nov. 29, 1996, when Thomas arrived with a shipment of goods—and a new associate, Carla Schrom. The only problem: Schrom was an undercover investigator, and this special delivery was a sting. Charges were dropped against everyone but Judy, who was fined $5,000 and who did nine days and 120 hours community service for attempting to receive stolen goods. In the end Thomas had shopped till he copped, turning in Judy to ensure his own freedom.

Gregory Thomas did much of his "shopping" at Burdines department store.

Glatzle baits the trap, posing as a potential mark on a dark side street.

Muggable Mary, Bane of Bad Guys

A fellow cop frisks the perp at the precinct. Another job well done.

SHE WAS MUGGED MORE THAN 300 TIMES—INCLUDING FIVE TIMES IN 24 hours in the summer of 1973. Ouch. Some perps pulled guns, some pulled knives, and one maniac went after her with a baseball bat. Like a real-life version of one of those kids' clown toys, Mary Glatzle, 33, kept popping back up for more—it was the bad guys who *really* got busted. Dressed as a homeless woman, a prostitute or even a bearded man, Glatzle, petite but fearless, was actually a New York City detective and dedicated decoy fondly known as Muggable Mary. "My friends think this is a glamorous job," she said one frigid night. But no matter the weather, she said, "you can't really keep gloves on your hands because—God forbid—you may need that gun."

Lt. Richard Conklin of Stamford, Conn., unfurls Patten's 20-foot rap sheet.

A SMOOTH OPERATOR, DRESSED FOR SUCCESS

PEOPLE BARELY NOTICED BRUCE PATTEN AS HE strode confidently through their corporate offices. True, no one actually knew him, but the guy was so well dressed and courteous that he simply *had* to be the business pro he claimed to be. He was a pro all right: Over 20 years Patten, 48 when he was caught in Stamford, Conn., in 1998, pulled off hundreds of robberies from coast to coast. His MO? He'd flash fake IDs and chat up receptionists until they let him pass, then wander the halls, ducking into empty offices to grab jewelry, wallets and checkbooks. He preferred nailing lawyers, though he began his career robbing homes in places like Beverly Hills. "He was known as the Gentleman Burglar," said Patten's attorney. "When he would go into a house, there would be absolutely nothing messed up. You almost had the feeling that if the people had left their bed unmade, he'd make it." A popular guy with the law, he was wanted in several cities and subsequently served time in California and Massachusetts.

A Vivid Dream Became a Nightmare

N STEVEN LINSCOTT'S DREAM, A BLOND MAN STOOD OVER A YOUNG woman and beat her to death. Linscott, 26, a psych major and supervisor of the Good News Mission in Oak Park, Ill., was disturbed by his vision, but sometimes had premonitions, so he thought it might prove useful to police.

They happened to be investigating the Oct. 3, 1980, killing of Karen Ann Phillips, 24, a nursing student at the Mission and, indeed, they found Linscott's tale intriguing—so much so that after repeated questioning they arrested him. Although there were discrepancies between Linscott's dream and reality, a jury convicted him of murder, and he was sentenced to 40 years in prison. The case went back and forth on appeal, with one court throwing out the conviction only to have the next reinstate it. In 1992, one week before Linscott's retrial was to begin, a new DNA test ruled him out, the charges were dropped, and he walked away a free man.

There was no evidence that Linscott ever met the victim, Karen Ann Phillips.

Patten had 15 stolen drivers licenses with him when he was nabbed.

SAN DIEGO HARBOR EXCURSION

APRIL 16 1998

Linscott (with his family) says he had upsetting dreams for weeks before the murder.

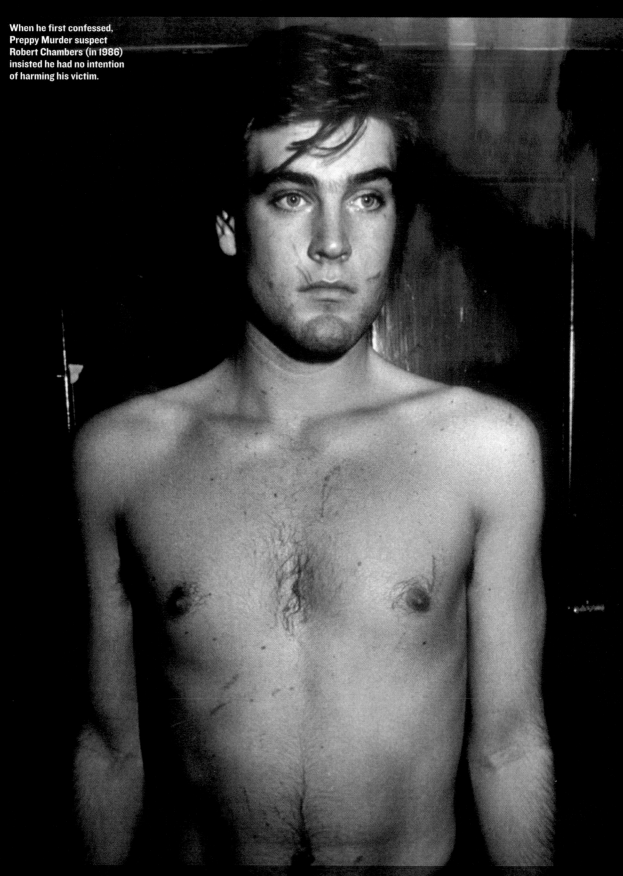

When he first confessed, Preppy Murder suspect Robert Chambers (in 1986) insisted he had no intention of harming his victim.

"I was really pissed off . . . I was in a frenzy . . . I didn't mean to hurt her. She was just too pushy. She molested me in the park."

ROBERT CHAMBERS

CRIMES OF PASSION

I ronically, few things create as much hatred—murderous hatred—as love. Specifically, damaged love: gone wrong, unrequited, impeded, obsessive. "Heaven has no rage like love to hatred turned," 17th-century author William Congreve famously wrote, "Nor hell a fury like a woman scorned." Update "woman" to "spouse" or "troubled ex-boyfriend," and Congreve could be a talking head on Court TV.

Passion can be both the root of the crime and the perp's state of mind: They often claim the mayhem wasn't planned but happened in a moment of irrational rage. That's what Betty Broderick said—after pumping five shots from a .38-cal. revolver into her ex-husband and his new wife in their bedroom. Jean Harris claimed she had meant to shoot herself but somehow—it gets complicated—shot her former lover, Scarsdale Diet guru Dr. Herman Tarnower, four times instead.

In both cases the jury wasn't buying.

TALL, DARK AND DEADLY: A PREPPY KILLER

A summer night, a singles bar, school about to begin. Jennifer Levin had a crush, but Robert Chambers was not what he seemed

"She had this softness, an aura of childlike innocence," a friend said of Levin. Chambers (below) demonstrated to police how he manhandled her during what tabloids later called "Wild Sex."

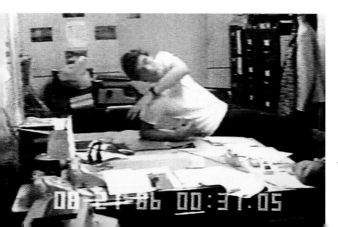

"FORGET ABOUT HIM," THE FATHERLY BAR owner cautioned Jennifer Levin when she confessed that she was smitten with Robert Chambers, a tall and handsome fellow prep-school grad whose troubles—authorities would later identify him as a drug user and burglar—were probably not apparent to Levin as she eyed him across the barroom. "You can do better than that," the owner counseled. "Before you get married, you'll have 20 different guys."

Two hours after Levin, 18, left the bar, Dorrian's Red Hand, with Chambers, 19, a bicyclist found her battered, half-naked body in a stand of trees behind the stately Metropolitan Museum of Art building in New York City's Central Park. Sitting across the street, watching, was Chambers, his face so badly scratched that he looked like he'd been in "an industrial accident," according to a witness. That explanation sounded more likely than the one Chambers gave police at first—that the numerous deep scratches that covered his face, chest and abdomen had been caused by a cat. And that the fresh wounds on his hands were from a mishap with a floor sander. In truth the 5'7", 135-lb. Levin had bloodied the 6'3", 200-lb. Chambers as she fought desperately to live.

A recent graduate of New York's exclusive Baldwin School, Levin was planning to leave for college in the fall. Celebrating summer's end with friends early on the morning of Aug. 26, 1986, she approached Chambers, with whom she had hooked up earlier that summer. The two had first met in the same bar when Chambers, who had recently been expelled from Boston University, told Levin that she, a friend later testified, was "the most beautiful girl I've ever seen."

Taken into custody by police later that day, Chambers admitted, after a seven-hour interrogation, that he had killed Levin—"accidentally" he insisted—during what he claimed began as mutually consensual but rough sex. "I didn't mean to hurt her," he said. "She was just too pushy. She molested me in the park."

Expressing remorse only for himself—a detective heard him complain to his father, "That f----- bitch! Why didn't she leave me alone?"—Chambers, and his lawyers, pursued the same blame-the-victim line of defense during his 1988 trial, a tactic

"Somebody died," a still unrepentant Chambers (in 1988) said in a 1998 parole hearing. "It was an accident."

that was almost universally condemned by the public, if not the deeply divided jury. "It was Jennifer who was pursuing Robert for sex," defense attorney Jack Litman said in closing arguments. "That's why we wound up with this terrible tragedy." Jennifer's sister was not alone in her reaction: "Litman killed her all over again."

UPDATE: Many thought Chambers got off easy when, to avoid a mistrial, he pleaded guilty to manslaughter, which could have allowed his release after five years in prison. Due to bad behavior, Chambers was released in 2003, after serving the maximum 15 years. Years later Jennifer's mother, Ellen, said that when she sees a woman in her 30s, "I think what Jennifer might be doing, what she would look like . . . And all that loss runs deep."

"Jennifer burst into beauty at 16," her heartbroken father recalled long after her body was found. "She was the girl next door."

Later an ordained minister, Bobbitt (in 1993) joked about starting the "Church Without an Organ."

"What I did wasn't right either," Lorena Bobbitt (in 1993) said of unmanning her then husband with a 12-inch knife (below). "But I was trying to defend myself."

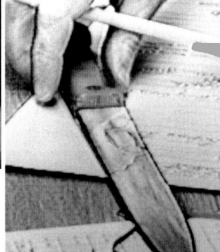

BOBBITT: THE UNKINDEST CUT

HE DIDN'T CARE ABOUT MY FEELings," said Lorena Bobbitt, explaining to police why she cut off her husband's penis, as he slept, with a kitchen carving knife and tossed it out the window of her car. (She also claimed he had sexually abused her.) Recovered by reluctant police officers, the bloody part was delivered to a local hospital, where doctors reattached the AWOL appendage to its grateful owner, ex-Marine turned Manassas, Va., bouncer John Wayne Bobbitt, 26, after nine hours of history-making microsurgery. Once the ensuing media storm, the one liners ("Every guy in America is sleeping on his stomach now," said Jay Leno) and lunacy (a Burbank radio station sponsored a Lorena Bobbitt Weenie Toss) subsided, there was more. While Lorena, 24, was found not guilty of malicious wounding by reason of insanity and returned to work as a manicurist, her ex followed his part into showbiz and became a porn star.

An Island Offered No Escape

"She wanted to get married and have a family," a friend recalled. When Beth met Toolan, "everyone was rooting for her."

WHEN BETH LOCHTEFELD MET FORMER WALL Street exec Tom Toolan, she thought she hit the love lotto. "She was giddy with excitement," recalled a friend. She was saying, 'He's so great; he's so smart; he's preppy.'" But Mr. Right couldn't have been more wrong. Beneath the Oxford cloth lurked what one woman who dated him called "a Jekyll and Hyde" personality. Beth, 44 and a successful New York City businesswoman who had recently moved to bucolic Nantucket island, apparently glimpsed Toolan's Hyde side. On Oct. 23, 2004, she spoke to police about a restraining order against Toolan, 37, who lived in New York, but she felt safe on the island and did not pursue the matter. Two days later Lochtefeld was discovered stabbed to death on her living room floor. According to police, Toolan had flown to Nantucket that morning and purchased a five-inch diving knife; a witness reportedly later saw him outside Beth's cottage. Arrested in Rhode Island, reportedly while driving drunk in a rented car, he pleaded not guilty during an arraignment in Massachusetts, where his trial was pending.

HATE LEAVES A MARK, BUT BEAUTY ENDURES

"Everyone has scars," Hanson said, putting on a brave face in '98. "Mine show."

SHE WAS SO PRETTY AND DELICATE," A fashion booking agent said of Marla Hanson. "Her features were so finely structured; her skin was beautiful. We just liked her right away." Those very attributes made the Missouri-born beauty a target of perverse desire. In an instant of nightmarish horror, Hanson, 24, was accosted on a Manhattan street by two men as she argued with her landlord Steven Roth, whose crude advances she had repeatedly rejected. As one man held her, the other slashed her face 15 times with a razor, cutting deep, disfiguring gashes. Eighteen years and numerous surgeries later, the scars, though faint, are still visible. Though disappointed that her two attackers and Roth, who hired the men (his motive, prosecutors said, was sexual rage over being rejected), served no more than 10 years each for assault, Hanson has found a large measure of happiness after years of despair. "People," says the married mother of one, "no longer define me only by my scar. It's just there and it doesn't mean anything."

A HEADMISTRESS PACKS HEAT

A love triangle proves to be a lethal recipe for the famed 'Scarsdale Diet' doc

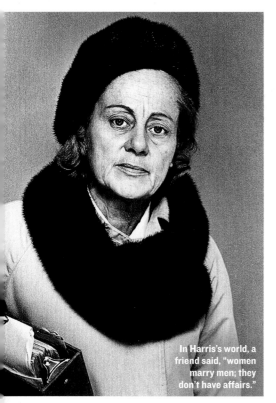

In Harris's world, a friend said, "women marry men; they don't have affairs."

AS SHE HAD MANY TIMES before, Jean Harris drove five hours from the exclusive Virginia girls' school, where she served as the prim, proper and oh-so-strict headmistress, to the New York estate of her longtime lover Dr. Herman Tarnower, best-selling author and creator of the so-called Scarsdale Diet. Distraught that her 14-year affair with Tarnower was ending, Harris, clad in mink, arrived with a bouquet of daisies in her hand and a .32-cal. Smith & Wesson revolver in her purse.

Late that night housekeepers summoned police. They arrived to find Tarnower, 69, dying on his bedroom floor from four bullet wounds, and a distraught Harris, then 57, preparing to flee the scene in a car with the murder weapon tucked in the glove compartment.

It seemed like an open-and-shut case. During the sensational 18-week murder trial that followed, prosecutors argued that a jealous Harris had driven from the Madeira School intent upon killing Tarnower rather than lose the unlikely lothario to a younger, prettier rival. Testimony that the cardiologist, known forever after by his nom de headline the "Diet Doc," was spending most nights with his assistant Lynne Tryforos, a 37-year-old divorced mother of two, and squiring her to the kind of dinners, parties and charity events that Harris had previously enjoyed, helped bolster their case. So did a letter Harris mailed to Tarnower on the morning of the murder. Calling Tryforos "a vicious, adulterous psychotic . . . your slut . . . your whore," Harris wrote that the doctor in turn made her feel "like a piece of old discarded garbage." Vowing to attend his upcoming 70th birthday, the headmistress—who would brook no such talk from the proper young ladies in her charge at Madeira—wrote that she would be there "even if the slut comes—indeed, I don't care if she pops naked out of a cake with her tits frosted chocolate."

There was no room for sweets in his diet plan, but the rest of the scenario might have held some appeal for Tarnower, who was known as a ladies' man, as well as a lover of fine cuisine, fine art and the kind of bragging rights that come with the big-game trophies that adorned the walls of his home. "I'm thinking of throwing a party and inviting all the women

Favorite dish: Tarnower included a recipe, "Spinach Delight à la Lynne," in his book as a tribute to Tryforos.

who are chasing me," the doctor had once told a friend. At one point he had proposed to Harris. He later backed out, and she returned his $50,000 ring—then acquiesced to the sort of romantic arrangement that she often condemned in others.

In the months before his murder, Tarnower stage-managed his simultaneous affairs with Harris and Tryforos, instructing his household staff to be sure to clear his bedroom of one woman's clothing and cosmetics when the other was expected for a visit. Of late, however, it appeared that the younger of his lovers held greater appeal to Tarnower, who told his staff to tell Harris he was not in should she call or visit while her rival was on the premises.

"It's all so contemptible," Harris told biographer Shana Alexander as details of the love triangle were revealed in court. A magna cum laude graduate of Smith College and a highly thought of prep school teacher before she became headmistress at Madeira, Harris, nicknamed "Integrity Jean" by students, told a friend, "I don't approve of all this sleeping around" at the school. "But she was doing it herself," said the friend. "She couldn't resolve that conflict." Added another: "She was getting older and she was desperate. Tarnower must have been her last chance. He looked like a lizard, but he had everything she wanted: money, a prestigious career, standing. If she let him go, that meant giving up her dreams."

Harris herself admitted as much. "I couldn't function as a useful human person anymore," she told Alexander, explaining why she drove to Tarnower's Westchester County, N.Y., estate: not to murder him, she claimed, but to kill herself—on the shores of a favorite pond on his property. Her plan went awry, she said, when she entered the house where the doctor was sleeping and, finding the "other woman's" nightgown in "my bathroom," she flew into a rage, shouting and throwing things.

According to the prosecution, she pumped two slugs into Tarnower as he lay in bed and two more as he tried to telephone for help. But Harris insisted that when the doctor awoke and found her in his room, he leapt from bed enraged and slapped her. A fight ensued, and the gun went off accidentally, as Tarnower tried to prevent her from turning it on herself, Harris testified. In the frenzy the doctor was hit four times, and when she realized he was seriously wounded, she claimed, she put the gun to her head, only to hear the hammer click on an empty chamber. As she examined the revolver to figure out why there were only five rounds in the chamber—she later realized that she had test fired it earlier, she claimed—Harris accidentally pulled the trigger again.

THE VERDICT: The jury concluded that it was Harris who went ballistic. Sentenced to 15 years to life, she was granted clemency by New York Gov. Mario Cuomo in 1992.

"Fellas, please!" Harris's lawyer admonished reporters besieging her. "You don't understand my client. She's very much a lady!"

THE FATAL ATTRACTION OF A FEMME FATALE

Carolyn Warmus (arriving at court in 1989) told Solomon in a note after his wife's death that he was "the most gorgeous man I've ever seen."

BETTY JEANNE AND PAUL Solomon were enjoying a quiet Sunday at home, leafing through pamphlets advertising retirement communities and contemplating their future together, when their reveries were interrupted by a phone call. Hours later Paul, having told his wife that he was going bowling, returned home to find Betty Jeanne, 40, sprawled on the living room floor, dead from bullet wounds.

At first Paul, 39, a sixth-grade teacher at Greenville Elementary School in suburban Westchester County, N.Y., was the prime suspect. But after a yearlong investigation, police arrested his colleague Carolyn Warmus, a pretty 26-year-old heiress with whom he had tried, none too strenuously, to break off an affair shortly before the murder. According to police it was Warmus who called Solomon at home on that afternoon in January 1989, persuading him to meet her for a drink that evening at a Holiday Inn bar called the Treetops Lounge. After waiting for Solomon to leave home, Warmus, police said, rang the bell of his apartment and opened fire, hit-

ting Betty Jeanne with a barrage of shots, including four in her back. Before the barrel could cool, Warmus joined her victim's unsuspecting husband at Treetops for champagne and oysters, then capped the evening with sex in the backseat of her car. "This *Fatal Attraction* stuff doesn't surprise me," a former University of Michigan sorority sister said. "She has always been going out with someone who's attached."

In fact Warmus, heir to a $107 million insurance fortune, had a history of obsessive behavior toward men. While an undergraduate at Michi-

With his adultery an issue, teacher Solomon evoked *The Scarlet Letter* in court.

gan, a teaching assistant she dated briefly obtained a court order to stop her from harassing him and his fiancée. Moving to New York City, where she earned her master's in education, she hired a detective to follow a married bartender who spurned her. "She was always very persistent," said a friend with a gift for understatement. "She didn't take rejection well."

Her 1991 murder trial was a tabloid sensation that featured a seedy private eye who had sold her the murder weapon and silencer for $2,500, juicy details about her trysts with Solomon in her apartment upstairs from Manhattan's Catch a Rising Star comedy club, and her reply when he asked her if she killed his wife: "Paul, I'm so glad you feel comfortable enough to ask me that." Not surprisingly, Solomon—who sold the rights to the story of his wife's killing to HBO for as much as $175,000 and carried on an affair with another young teacher in the aftermath of his wife's death— was asked to temporarily cease molding young minds at Greenville Elementary after parents petitioned to have him fired.

THE VERDICT: Warmus, whose inheritance evaporated due to her father's legal troubles, is serving 25 years to life in Bedford Hills, N.Y., for second-degree murder. The prison is about 30 miles from the site of the former Treetops Lounge.

"If there had not been *The Jenny Jones Show*, Scott Amedure [above] would be alive," a relative said.

Jenny Jones & the Chat Show Murder

SOMETHING STRANGE AND WONDERFUL HAS HAPPENED TO me," Jon Schmitz told his parents shortly before his appearance on *The Jenny Jones Show*. A Michigan waiter with a history of emotional problems, he later said that producers told him only that he would be meeting a secret admirer. They did not mention, he later claimed, that the 1995 segment was titled "Secret Crushes on People of the Same Sex." Full of anticipation when he stepped out onstage during the show's live taping, he was more than surprised, he said, to find his secret admirer was not the woman he had hoped for but 32-year-old Scott Amedure, a good-humored *Jenny Jones* fan who confessed his desire to slather Schmitz, 26, in "whipped cream and champagne."

Unamused, Schmitz came calling on Amedure three days later, toting a shotgun. After firing twice at point-blank range, Schmitz called 911 and confessed, telling the operator, "He f----- me on national TV."

Emotional problems led Schmitz (en route to court in 1995) to twice attempt suicide.

THE VERDICT: Schmitz, who feared the show (which never aired) would make people "think I'm gay," is serving 25 to 50 years for second-degree murder.

SCORNED—AND SEETHING

When her husband left her for a younger woman, ex-trophy wife Betty Broderick settled differences with a nickel-plated revolver

UPON LEARNING THAT HER HUSBAND OF 14 YEARS, HIGH-POW-ered San Diego attorney Dan Broderick, was having an affair with a legal assistant 15 years his junior, his wife, like many a wronged woman before her, gathered up his clothing, including some of his best custom-made suits, and threw them into the backyard. Not content with a merely symbolic act, however, Elisabeth "Betty" Broderick further vented her rage by dousing the exquisitely tai-lored duds in gasoline and setting them ablaze. The expensive bon-fire would later be seen as the opening salvo in what friends and acquaintances of the couple would call a real-life *War of the Roses*, the 1989 Michael Douglas-Kathleen Turner black comedy about a couple whose unciv-il war is fought to the death. Following a brief truce, the Broderick battles began to escalate in 1985, when Dan moved out and filed for divorce. That year Betty entered the house where Dan was living temporarily and spray-painted the walls black. After she smeared a cream pie over his belongings and smashed a window with an umbrella, Dan pressed charges and, according to Betty's lawyer, proceeded, without her knowledge, to empty their bank accounts and sell the home they once shared.

The animosity—and violence—ratcheted higher in 1986, when Bet-ty rammed her car into the front door of Dan's new home in an exclusive San Diego suburb. As he confronted her, Dan saw through the car window that there was a butcher knife on the front seat by his ex-wife's side. Before police arrived, Betty slugged Dan on the head with a brass key ring, and he retaliated by punching her in the stomach. As a result of the melee,

"The guy asked me to marry him every day for three years," Betty said of Dan (in 1969). "He promised me the moon."

Betty spent three days in a county mental hospital for observation. When the couple's divorce was finalized in August 1986, she was denied custody of their four children. Awarded a Jaguar, an oceanview home in La Jolla and $16,000 per month in alimony, Betty remained bitterly resentful of her ex. "He drove me crazy," she later said of Dan, whose announced plans to wed his former legal assistant Linda Kolkena apparently caused the estranged couple's battle to take a deadly turn.

In March 1989, Betty purchased a .38-cal. Smith & Wesson revolver and,

according to Dan's sister Kathy, cleaned the weapon as sons Rhett, then 10, and Danny, 13, two of the warring Brodericks' four collaterally damaged children, looked on. "It's what I'm going to use to kill your father," she said matter of factly.

Twenty years earlier she and Dan had exchanged far more tender vows. Wed in 1969, the clean-cut and ambitious pair strove, Betty later said, for "wealth, social standing, a large family." A decade later Dan, who had degrees in both medicine and law, was earning a million a year, and Betty seemed happy as a stay-at-home mom. But fissures became apparent as Dan devoted much of his time to work rather than family. Betty, according to daughter Kim, responded with vindictive and increasingly erratic behavior. "I didn't like that Dad got restraining orders against her," Kim said. "But what could he do? When he tried to deal with her, she screamed obscenities."

Fearing much worse, Dan hired security guards to prevent his ex from crashing his April 1989 wedding to Kolkena, who begged him to wear a bulletproof vest for the nuptials. He refused and the ceremony and reception took place without incident.

Seven months later, in the pre-dawn hours of Nov. 5, 1989, Betty Broderick entered Dan's Marston Hills home, using a key that belonged to one of their children. Confronting her ex in the master bedroom, where Dan, 44, and his bride, 28, slept, she opened fire. The new Mrs. Broderick died instantly of gunshot wounds to the neck and chest. Dan died minutes later, his lung pierced by a slug. Betty, who said she had gone to the house not to kill the victims but to shoot herself—"I wanted to splash my brains all over his goddamned house," she said—was confronted two days later by Kim, who would testify against her in two trials. "She told me, 'We'll be happy now,'" Kim said. "She didn't feel bad at all."

"He traded me in for a younger model and stole my kids," Betty said two years later, as she was about to stand trial for the second time (an earlier trial ended in a hung jury). At both trials her defense was that she was an emotionally battered woman. "He sued me to death . . . My story is relevant to millions of women."

Enough so that her case became a cause célèbre, spawned a hit made-for-TV movie that drew 28 million viewers in 1992 and inspired a sequel that was broadcast later that year with a tie-in appearance taped in jail for *The Oprah Winfrey Show*. "I have regrets, not remorse," Betty told PEOPLE. "I regret my husband had no character, that my children lost their mother, home and stability. I didn't do the legal bullying. I wasn't the one who had the affair. I won't accept the blame for what happened." To reporters she remained unrepentant: "The f----- is dead," Betty said of Dan. "He's cold to the wind."

THE TRIAL: Convicted on two counts of second-degree murder in 1991, Betty was sentenced to a minimum of 17½ years in prison.

Betty remained "in good spirits" during her trial, friends said. "I don't mind at all," she said of her daily prison chores.

GIMME AN "M": THE TEXAS CHEERLEADER MURDER PLOT

WHEN IT CAME TO HER daughter Shanna's making the cheerleading team, Wanda Holloway knew that it was popularity, not pom poms, that counted. She encouraged Shanna to actively campaign for a spot on her Channelview, Texas, junior high school squad by handing out free pencils and rulers embossed with her name to rally support. Unfortunately such politicking was verboten, and Shanna was disqualified when a rival's mom blew the whistle.

When Shanna was taunted in the hallways for her failure, her mom seethed with anger and plotted revenge against her daughter's nemesis, cheerleader Amber Heath, and her meddling mother, Verna. "That's all she ever talked about," said one of Wanda's ex-inlaws. "She'd go on and on about it to anybody who'd listen."

"Yes, I have some hatred and meanness," admitted Wanda (below), whose misdeeds were chronicled in HBO's 1993 cult hit *The Positively True Adventures of the Alleged Texas Cheerleader-Murdering Mom*, "but I am not a vengeful-type person." Amber (above), once friendly with Shanna (left, at a school banquet in 1991), might disagree.

Wanda's ex-brother-in-law Terry Harper heard her loud and clear. A matrimonially challenged former petty criminal who couldn't recall if he had been married six or seven times, Harper suggested—jokingly, he claimed—that she have Verna killed. When Wanda later asked him if he knew how to arrange such a hit, Terry went to the cops, who fitted him with a wire. During one conversation that must have made countless officer hours spent listening to dull surveillance tapes seem worthwhile, Terry balked at the suggestion that Amber be rubbed out as well. "But Terry, you don't know this little girl," Wanda said. "Ooh! I can't stand her. I mean, she's a bitch. Makes me sick. I mean, I could knock her in the face, you know?"

Deciding that the $7,500 it would cost to have both mother and daughter knocked off was too steep, Wanda agreed to pay $2,500 for a hit on Verna. Then, seemingly giddy with excitement over the prospect of ridding the world of Verna, Wanda asked Terry about the nonexistent triggerman he'd lined up for the hit. "This guy, badass or what?" Terry's reply—"Yeah, yeah, he's bad to the bone, baby"—was good enough for Wanda, who sealed the deal with a pair of $2,000 diamond earrings and was promptly arrested for solicitation of capital murder. Weeping at her trial, she said, "I never wanted Verna killed, or Amber, ever. I'm sorry I said all that stuff. I know it sounds awful."

THE VERDICT: In 1996 Holloway was sentenced to 10 years, with 6 months in prison and 9½ years on probation.

Burning Down the House

"I'm not looking forward to seeing the movie," Francine (below) said of NBC's 1984 blockbuster *The Burning Bed*, inspired by her case and starring Farrah Fawcett (above).

ORN UNDER A BAD SIGN AND WORSE—A FATHER WHO GAMBLED, drank and beat her mother—Francine Moran thought she had found an escape from her troubled home in hardscrabble Jackson, Mich., in the person of 18-year-old Mickey Hughes. "I thought he was so sophisticated," she said of the taciturn high school dropout and day laborer whom she had wed at 16 in 1963. "He had his own car and most people I knew didn't."

Hughes had wheels all right, and he spent his life spinning them. Drifting through a series of dead-end jobs, he often blew his earnings on drinking binges and took out his frustrations on Francine, beating her through the births of her four children. "Sometimes it would last for hours, or sometimes for just a few minutes and he would leave and go to the bar. Then he would come back and start again," Francine said. "I learned that if I fought back, it only made him more angry. I thought, well, maybe I could kill myself. But then I thought if I kill myself, who is going to take care of the kids? Nobody could love them like me."

Finally, on March 9, 1977, after a long day of beatings and humiliations, Francine poured gasoline around the bed where Hughes slept in a drunken stupor, lit a match and ran outside as the fire consumed the entire house and her tormentor along with it. Before firefighters arrived, she sped away in her blue Ford Granada and drove straight to the local jail, where she hysterically confessed, "I did it!" Francine was tried for murder, but a sympathetic jury found her not guilty by reason of temporary insanity.

THE MOMENT: "I was thinking about all the things that had happened to me . . . all the times he had hurt me . . . how he had hurt the kids. I stood still for a moment, hesitating, and a voice urged me on. It whispered, 'Do it! Do it! Do it!'"

MURDER BY MERCEDES: FUELED BY JEALOUSY

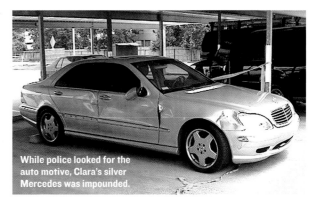

While police looked for the auto motive, Clara's silver Mercedes was impounded.

HE HOTEL STAFF WATCHED IN HORROR AS A MELEE that started in the lobby spilled out into the entranceway. Clara Harris had driven to the hotel to confront her husband, David, whom she suspected of having an affair. When David and his girlfriend Gail Bridges, an employee in one of the Houston-area dental offices that the Harrises owned, stepped off the elevator together, Clara assaulted her rival. "I saw her pulling and screaming at Gail," recalled a desk clerk, who helped separate the women and escorted Bridges, whose shirt had been torn from her back, outside, with a dazed David following. Hurrying to her Mercedes, Clara started it up, aimed it at David and "burned rubber," a witness said, effectively turning the car, a prosecutor would later say, into "a 4,000-lb. murder weapon." After striking him once, according to a witness, she circled around and ran over him three more times before backing over his body once for good measure. Another witness said Clara next ran to her husband and, cradling his bloody head, sobbed, "David, are you okay?"

And there lay the quandary for jurors in her 2003 trial: Did she maliciously and with forethought murder her husband? Or was she caught up in a rage of such blind fury that she didn't know what she was doing?

Practicing dentists and the parents of twin 4-year-old sons, Clara and David, both 44, had seemed ideally suited. When Clara first got wind of his affair, she was so desperate to please him, she even contemplated liposuction and breast implants. "Her whole life," said a friend, "was keeping David."

Two surprising supporters? Her in-laws, who hoped she would receive two years in prison for the lesser charge of criminally negligent homicide. "We love her; we want her to be with her boys," said David's father. "That's our stance and we are going to hold it. We are trying to do the best we can for our family."

A 2001 ad promoted the Harrises' practices.

THE VERDICT: Convicted of murder, she was sentenced to 20 years in prison.

Friends of Villegas (in 1998) were "outraged and saddened" by the verdict.

CRIME AND PUNISHMENT AMONG THE HORSE SET

HANDSOME AND DASHING, WITH A DAZZLING GRIN AND STAR-quality athletic gifts, polo pro Roberto Villegas found that his prowess with the ponies was matched by his way with women. "He was a nice guy, but he messed around," a colleague said of Villegas, a farmer's son from Argentina, whose skill on the polo grounds took him from poverty to the moneyed estates of Virginia's horse country. "Everyone knew," an acquaintance said of rumors that Villegas was cheating on his girlfriend, billionheiress Susan Cummings. "He wasn't being very cool about it."

Nor, seemingly, was Cummings, the 35-year-old daughter of a wealthy arms dealer. When police arrived at her 339-acre estate in Warrenton, Va., an enclave for the ultrarich, on Sept. 7, 1997, they found Villegas, 38, dead from four gunshot wounds. Prosecutors would later say that Cummings killed her lover in a jealous rage. But the heiress told PEOPLE in a pretrial interview that the killing was in self-defense. While it was confirmed that she had taken steps to obtain a restraining order prior to the killing, her case seemed weak until three witnesses said they had each seen Villegas hit

"I felt, 'This is it. This man is going to kill me,'" said Cummings, who said she fired four shots in a panic.

or choke Cummings. Testifying in her own defense, the heiress said she fired a burst from an automatic weapon "in a moment of desperation" after he lunged at her with a knife. Sympathetic jurors bought the story and convicted her of the lesser charge of voluntary manslaughter. "We couldn't stand Roberto after all he had done to Susan," said a juror. When the heiress was then sentenced to 60 days in jail and fined $2,500, courthouse veterans were incredulous: "You could get five years in Virginia for killing a horse," said one.

Joey Buttafuoco (at home in 1992) would later serve six months for statutory rape.

L'Affaire Buttafuoco

MARY JO BUTTAFUOCO WAS out on the back deck cleaning lawn furniture when the doorbell rang. The stranger at the door—a pretty, petite teenager with dark, violet-tinted hair—told Mary Jo that her husband was having an affair with an unnamed teen. A worldly 37-year-old blonde, Mary Jo listened calmly, thanked the girl for stopping by and nonchalantly turned to go back inside. Before she could reach the screen door, the girl, 17-year-old Amy Fisher, pulled out a .25-cal. Titan pistol and fired a single shot. The bullet severed the carotid artery in Mary Jo's neck, destroyed her right eardrum and lodged, permanently, in the base of her skull. Fisher ran from the front porch, leaving her victim for dead, and sped away in a waiting Thunderbird with an acquaintance at the wheel.

So began the lurid saga of the Long Island Lolita. The stars: Fisher, a senior at John F. Kennedy High School in Bellmore, N.Y., who worked after school and weekends as a hooker for

Amy said, "'He loves me. We have great sex,'" a friend said. "It's all she talked about. Joey, Joey, Joey"

"This is not your typical 17-year-old high school student," the judge was told in court.

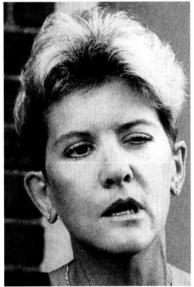

"[Our] story is pretty simple," Mary Jo said. "I love my Joey and my Joey loves me."

a local escort service (customers could summon her from classes via her "007" beeper code), and Joey Buttafuoco, an auto-body repair-shop owner whose name would become a catchword immortalized by such comedians as David Letterman, who invokes it to this day. Mary Jo herself nearly stole the show. She not only survived to stand by her man,

but she proved herself impervious to embarrassment as well as bullets, repeatedly chatting on-air with Howard Stern about her and Joey's sex life and never hesitating to show her wounds on-camera or walk news crews through the crime scene at her waterfront home in Massapequa, N.Y.

Among the other standouts in the long-playing saga was Fisher's lawyer, a former vibrating-bed salesman who tried to raise his client's $2 million bail by selling rights to her life story to the highest bidder. The parade of shady characters included coworkers at the ABBA escort service, who said they knew Buttafuoco as a pimp and coke dealer they called "Joey Coco Pops." One of Fisher's customers secretly videotaped his sex romp with her, then sold the tape to *A Current Affair* for $7,500. An acquaintance of Amy's admitted accepting oral sex as payment for staking out the Buttafuoco home, and another said he sold her the Titan for $800 cash but was disappointed that she didn't sweeten the deal with sex.

Along with consuming forests of newsprint and proving tabloid TV's crowning glory, the Amy Fisher sto-

ry generated three TV movies, four books and an Off-Broadway musical.

SURPRISE BENEFACTOR: Sentenced to 5 to 15 years after pleading guilty to attempted murder, Fisher (now married, the mother of two and a newspaper columnist) was released in 1999, after seven years served, thanks in part to a plea for leniency filed by none other than her victim, Mary Jo Buttafuoco.

Fisher (in '04) asked Mary Jo to write the intro to her book. Her victim refused.

When Dutch novelist Richard Klinkhamer admitted how he killed his wife, it was as if one of his dark novels had come to life.

"When I woke, I was in the tub surfacing from a horrible nightmare . . . . My clothes were on the floor, all bloodied. I got scared, felt the crazy urge to hide myself. No matter how intoxicated I still was, the consequences of my deed were as clear to me as if I had sobered in an instant." **FROM THE REWORKED MANUSCRIPT** *MINCE*

WEDNESDAY, RICHARD KLINKHAMER'S ACCOUNT OF HOW HE MIGHT HAVE KILLED HIS WIFE

STRANGER THAN PULP FICTION

Y ou read the book, you saw the movie, you loved them both. They were outrageous, unpredictable. And after the credits rolled, you said to yourself, "Great, loved it, but no way that happens in real life." Then you turned on the news. Somewhere, right between the Group of Seven Economic Summit wrap-up and Mr. Chippy with the local weather, there was a small, strange news item: A woman in Maryland was accused of poisoning her husband—during a Murder Mystery Weekend. Or maybe you saw the one about a woman charged with assaulting her (highly allergic) husband—with perfume. Or, chillingly, the piece about the woman killed on a deserted road by the one man no one suspected—a highway patrolman.

This may be the stuff that even a gifted novelist could never get away with—but it happens.

MURDER, HE WROTE

Dutch author Richard Klinkhamer was known for his grim novels.
But they paled in comparison to his murderous real-life saga

RACTICALLY FROM THE MOMENT RICHARD KLINK-hamer reported his wife missing on Feb. 6, 1991, neighbors were suspicious. Since Klinkhamer lost the couple's money in the 1987 stock market crash and took to drink, Hannie, 43, had sometimes shown up at neighbors' homes with bruises on her face. Police held Klinkhamer for a few days as they searched the area around his home in Finsterwolde, the Netherlands. Finding nothing, they released him.

Two years later Klinkhamer, the author of four dark novels, began touting a new manuscript, *Mince Wednesday,* in which he described ways that he *could* have killed Hannie, had he wanted to. "Villagers say I cut her into pieces," he told one intrigued TV interviewer. And that might have been that—until Klinkhamer sold his house. The buyers tore down the tool shed, ripped up its concrete floor and found what was lat-er identified as Hannie's jawbone. Arrested, Klinkhamer admitted he had killed Hannie, later explaining to PEOPLE that they had gotten into an argument. "She tried to hit me," he said. "Maybe I laughed; she hated that when she was mad at me. Suddenly the wrench that had been lying on the washer was in her hand." In the struggle he killed her.

THE VERDICT: Klinkhamer was sentenced to six years, and *Mince Wednesday* was never published.

Former neighbor Harry Weites points out the spot where Hannie's body lay concealed for eight years.

Hannie and Klinkhamer (above) were once very much in love, friends said. Margreet de Heer (left), his girlfriend at the time of his arrest, said he was reworking *Mince Wednesday* in jail as a way of "honoring" his dead wife.

"You're Pretty. I'm Gonna Keep You"

"I'd die to see a grizzly bear," Kari Swenson, an international star in the women's biathlon, said the day before she was kidnapped in the woods by two mountain men.

IT BEGAN WITH A GRIZZLY BEAR. KARI SWENSON, 23, AN international biathlete and part-time waitress at the Lone Mountain Ranch in the Madison Mountains in southwest Montana, had heard that a grizzly was sighted nearby and wanted to take a look for herself. She had hiked a couple of miles when she happened onto a campsite with sleeping bags. At that moment Don Nichols, 53, a self-described mountain man, and his son Danny, 19, a high school dropout, emerged from the woods. They looked her over and decided to keep her.

That happened in the early afternoon on July 15, 1984. When Kari didn't show for work by 5, friends, afraid that she might have been attacked by the grizzly, formed a search party. Walking along a creek the next morning, Jim Schwalbe and Alan Goldstein heard a rifle shot. Schwalbe ran and suddenly stopped cold: Nichols, the mountain man, held a gun on him while his son leaned over Kari, who had been chained in a sleeping bag to a tree. "I'm shot; help me," she cried out as Danny muttered, "Oh God, I didn't mean to shoot her."

As Schwalbe rushed over to treat Kari's wound, Goldstein stepped out of the forest, spoke quickly into a walkie-talkie, then whipped a pistol out of his backpack and ordered Nichols to drop his rifle. "Then bang," recalled Schwalbe, "Al was down, flat, just like that." Schwalbe raced to his side but saw that Al was dead so kept running. The last he heard of Nichols was his shouting, "Get that chain off her and shut up, Danny."

Schwalbe brought back help, and as Kari was airlifted by helicopter to a local hospital, the posse began a hunt, weapons raised, that lasted until dark. Day after day, searchers probed the valleys, hills and forests around Lone Mountain but failed to turn up the two men who had dropped out of society to live off the land.

Kari survived and recovered. Startled when he heard Schwalbe and Goldstein, Danny had accidentally pulled the trigger and shot Kari in the chest, just below her collarbone. She had kept her cool when Donald and Danny fled, crawling to Goldstein's backpack and eating a candy bar she found to help keep up her strength. She told police that the older man was sick and had vomited several times, and that the boy seemed to feel guilty about having kidnapped her. Once when Nichols was off in the woods, she asked the boy to let her go. He thought about it for a minute, then said, "No, you're pretty. I'm gonna keep you."

WHAT HAPPENED: Five months later, tipped off by a rancher who saw campfire smoke, Sheriff Johnny France tracked down the Nicholses. France strode into their camp and, deadpan, asked, "See any coyotes around?" When Don went for his gun, France warned, "Please don't make me kill you." Donald was sentenced to 85 years for murder and Danny served 6 years for his role in kidnapping Swenson.

MURDER IN A CAPSULE

Killing her husband wasn't enough, so Stella Nickell poisoned a perfect stranger

After Sue Snow was poisoned, stores emptied shelves of capsule-style painkillers.

P AUL WEBKING GRABBED A COUPLE OF EXTRA-STRENGTH Excedrin for his arthritis and kissed his sleepy wife, Sue Snow, goodbye. "I always told her I loved her," he said later. At about 6 a.m., Snow, 40, roused herself from bed and began getting ready for her job as an assistant vice president at a branch of the Puget Sound National Bank, just down the road from the couple's Auburn, Wash., home. As was her morning habit, she took two Excedrin capsules, counting on their caffeine content to give her an early morning boost. When Snow's daughter Hayley, 15, came looking for her mother a few minutes later, she found her on the bathroom floor. Paramedics rushed her to the hospital, but by noon Snow was dead.

Snow's family was bewildered—and even more baffled when they learned she had been poisoned. The Excedrin capsules Snow had taken were laced with cyanide, and somehow Paul had escaped the same fate.

It was not the first time someone had tampered with over-the-counter drugs. In 1982 seven people in Chicago died from cyanide-laced Tylenol. The murders were never solved, and investigators in Snow's case thought they might have a copycat killer on their hands.

Stella Nickell lived not far from Snow and Webking, and she was not a happy camper. She was in her 40s and living in a trailer with Bruce, 52, her second husband, a heavy equipment operator who used to drink too much but who Stella thought was even more of a bore when he stopped. Stella's needy elderly mother lived next door, and her daughter Cynthia from a previous marriage was divorced and had taken temporary refuge with Stella. Space and money were tight, and she was feeling increasingly hemmed in. If only she had some money, she told people, she could open a tropical-fish store. Stella loved tropical fish.

At first Cynthia didn't take her mother seriously when she said she could solve the family's problems if she killed her husband, made it look like an accident and collected the insurance money. Stella had taken out a $40,000 policy on Bruce, plus she knew he had a $31,000 state employee's policy that would kick in an additional $105,000 if his

Stella and husband Bruce (above) posed together in 1981. Paul Webking (right) holds a photo of his wife, Sue, Stella's second victim.

death were accidental. Ready to take the next step, Stella checked out library books about poison and made her move. After secretly dosing Bruce with either foxglove or hemlock, she waited to watch him writhe in agony. Instead, he said he felt kind of tired and that was it.

Then on June 5, 1986, Bruce came home from work, kissed his wife, and, complaining of a headache, grabbed a bottle of Excedrin and took four pills. He watched a little TV, went to his patio and minutes later shouted, "I feel like I'm going to pass out." He died a few hours later at the hospital. The coroner ruled that Bruce had died of pulmonary emphysema, so the insurance company refused to pay the $105,000 bonus for an accidental death. And that got Stella to thinking again.

Six days after Bruce's death, Sue Snow, who lived about 12 miles from Stella, bought a bottle of Excedrin from a local store, took a couple of capsules and died. This time the coroner detected poison. When Stella suggested to authorities that her husband might have died the same way, new tests proved her right, and she, like Snow's husband, filed a wrongful death suit against Bristol Myers, the makers of Excedrin.

Police thought Stella had planted the tainted Excedrin bottles in local stores but couldn't dig up enough convincing evidence incriminating her—until Cynthia, claiming she was suffering from a guilty conscience, came forward. How could Stella be so callous as to kill her own husband? On the stand during Stella's trial, Cynthia explained that Stella wasn't having a whole lot of fun anymore. She added that Stella "was very pleased that [Bruce] stopped drinking, but she didn't like it that he didn't do anything anymore."

THE VERDICT: Guilty of causing a death by tampering with a commercial product, Stella got 90 years.

Lynda Taylor's husband, David, said he lived "in fear" of her alleged aroma attacks. His allergies, she said, meant "we didn't get many visitors."

Caution!
A VERY CHEMICALLY SENSITIVE (ALLERGIC) PERSON LIVES HERE

DO NOT COME IN THE HOUSE IF YOU ARE WEARING: PERFUME, HAIR SPRAY, DEODORANT, OR DRY CLEANED CLOTHES.

NO SMOKING ON PREMISES

DO NOT EVEN KNOCK IF YOU HAVE WORKED IN OR AROUND STRONG CHEMICALS IN THE LAST 24 HOURS. (PESTICIDES, HERBICIDES, CLEANING SERVICES, PETRO CHEMICALS, PAINT THINNER, ETC.)

Law & Odor: The Smell of Assault

AVID TAYLOR KNEW SOMETHING WAS UP. HE COULD, LITERally, smell it. In the spring of 2003, his wife, Lynda, 36, began using scented air fresheners and scattering lavender sachets around their Jensen Beach, Fla., house. He said she even sprayed Lysol in his face. Which, for David, 46, was like getting Maced: He told police that Lynda knew he was allergic to many scents and he was subsequently suffering headaches and numbness. Worse, he claimed, she was trying to kill him because he wanted a divorce and she didn't like the way he proposed dividing the assets. "She never said, 'I am killing you,'" said David. "But she did say, 'Soon you won't be here.'" Lynda countered that her high-strung husband made their home life unbearably tense and that she began using lavender because she read it had a calming effect. After police sniffed around, Lynda went to trial on a misdemeanor battery charge and was acquitted. Oh, and Lynda and David split up.

A popular honor student at San Diego State, Knott "was always smiling," recalled a family friend.

The Killer Wore a Badge

SHORTLY AFTER 8 P.M., CARA Knott, 20, phoned from her boyfriend's place in Escondido, Calif., to let her parents know she was headed home to El Cajon. It was only a 45-minute drive, but by 10, Cara—a student at San Diego State University—hadn't arrived. Worried, her father, Sam, initiated a family manhunt. He and his wife, Joyce, drove up and down Interstate 15 and found nothing. At dawn the next morning, Dec. 28, 1986, Cara's sister Cynthia and brother-in-law Bill Weick decided to take a closer look at the Mercy Road off-ramp, an unfinished road that led to a shadowy pit beneath the highway. There, just past construction roadblocks, they spotted Cara's white VW. But Cara was nowhere to be found.

Later, as police combed the area, an officer peered over the railing of a bridge nearby and saw a young woman's body lying in a creek bed 65 feet below. In light of the tragedy, a local radio station aired an announcement featuring highway patrolman Craig Peyer and warning anyone with car troubles to stay in their vehicles. "You never know who you could meet," he cautioned.

Police quickly determined that Cara had been strangled. But the clues were perplexing. She had not been sexually assaulted. Her car had plenty of gas, was in fine working order, and the passenger side door was locked. Even though it had been a chilly evening, the driver's side window was partially rolled down. Police wondered why Cara had stopped her car in the first place. Then it hit them: Maybe she had stopped for someone she had reason to trust—a cop.

Checking duty reports, investigators found that Peyer, 38, a 13-year veteran of the force, had himself patrolled that stretch of road and issued a citation. He was known for writing an inordinately large number of tickets. Zeroing in on Peyer, police found a drop of blood on Cara's boot that was consistent with Peyer's, as well as a microscopic gold fiber on her sweatshirt that was consistent with Peyer's shoulder patch.

After Peyer's arrest, more than 20 women came forward to describe how he had pulled them over for minor traffic violations along that same stretch of highway and kept them for a half hour or longer asking sometimes disturbingly private questions. None accused him of making overtures, but several said they grew uncomfortable. "I think he liked pulling young women over and being the authority figure," said one woman. "He was a gentleman, but the longer he kept me . . . the more nervous I got."

THE VERDICT: Peyer was convicted of first-degree murder and sentenced to 25 years to life in prison.

Highway Patrolman Peyer was known around the precinct as a "hot pencil" because he issued as many as 250 traffic citations a month.

THE TOXICOLOGIST WHO BROUGHT HER WORK HOME

PARAMEDICS, SUMMONED BY A FRANTIC Kristin Rossum, found her husband, Greg de Villers, 26, dead on the floor of their La Jolla, Calif., home. A photo of their wedding lay beside him, and his body was sprinkled with rose petals—a possible cryptic reference to the film *American Beauty,* in which the star is killed. Rossum suggested he had taken two of her prescription drugs, and the case was ruled a suicide.

Kristin and Greg were all smiles on their wedding day

Friends and family thought otherwise, and urged police to take another look. When they did, they found that Greg's body was also awash with the potent pain killer fentanyl. Large amounts of fentanyl happened to be missing from the medical examiner's office where Rossum, 26, a toxicologist, worked—and had become romantically involved with her boss. Finally, there was the tell-tale receipt: On the day Greg died, Nov. 6, 2000, Rossum bought a single red rose at a local grocery store. The jury took less than eight hours to convict, and Rossum was sentenced to life.

Police said Rossum had a drug problem that she tried to conceal.

Madness Returns

NO QUESTION MICHAEL LAUDOR HAD INNER demons; the remarkable thing was how well he had tamed them. A Yale graduate, he began experiencing symptoms of schizophrenia in the mid-1980s, while working for a management consulting firm. The delusions quickly got worse, and he was forced to quit his job.

Rather than give up, Laudor sought treatment and slowly began to regain control over his life. Impressed with his own progress, he became determined to help others and opened a counseling program in suburban New York City to help people with physical and emotional disabilities. "He had accomplished a great deal, and that was worth sharing," said his partner in the project.

The New York Times hailed his recovery in a 1995 profile that caught the eye of Scribner's, which offered him a $600,000 book contract to tell his remarkable tale. Filmmaker Ron Howard bought the movie rights for another $1.5 million. Maybe best of all, Laudor fell in love and proposed to fellow Yale grad Caroline Costello, a technology specialist with a private firm that managed public schools.

"It seemed as if he had life by the tail," a friend said of the progress Laudor had made in overcoming schizophrenia.

Laudor used part of his windfall to buy a flat in Hastings, N.Y., where he began work on his book, which he titled *The Laws of Madness.* Perhaps it was the solitary nature of his work or the pain of recalling troubling times, but Laudor once again began to suffer symptoms of his illness. Already complaining that his medications were no longer effective, he was devastated and fell into a deep depression when his beloved father died of prostate cancer.

On the afternoon of June 17, 1998, police received a frantic call from Laudor's mother, Ruth, urging them to rush to her son's apartment. She had spoken with him several times that day and feared that his relapse was so complete he might become violent.

They were too late. Police found Laudor's fiancée, Costello, 37, lifeless on the kitchen floor, stabbed a dozen times. Even more heartbreaking, subsequent tests revealed that she was one-month pregnant with their first child. Later that night, in a moment of lucidity, Laudor, 35, turned himself in.

WHAT HAPPENED: The murder charge was dropped, and Laudor was sent to a psychiatric institution.

"It was like jumping from comedy to tragedy," said actress Bobbi Benitez (left, with the cast of the *The Bride Who Cried*).

A Deadly Drama Unfolds on Murder Mystery Weekend

E VENTS UNFOLDED QUICKLY. HAVING ALREADY SAMPLED A BIT OF THE bubbly, the happy groom raised his glass again in a toast. Then, with about 170 guests watching, he suddenly froze and pitched forward. It took only a couple of hours for police to make an arrest, cuffing the mother-in-law and charging her with murder for having poisoned the victim's champagne.

At that point the witnesses applauded. Resurrected, the groom even stood to take a bow. It was, after all, just good fun—murder mystery night at the Harbourtowne Golf Resort on Maryland's Eastern Shore, where the good and bad guys were really actors performing *The Bride Who Cried*.

Then a few hours later, a real mystery began. At about 1:30 a.m. on the morning of Feb. 15, 1998, Kim Hricko, 32, a resort guest from Laurel, Md., strolled

calmly up to the reception desk and said, "I think my room is on fire." Asked if anyone was still in the room, Hricko replied, "Yes, I think my husband is."

An employee and a guest sprinted to Hricko's cottage, where they found Stephen Hricko, 35, a burly golf course superintendent, uncon-

scious on his bed, his torso and head badly burned by a blaze that had consumed part of the mattress before sputtering out. They pulled him outside to safety, but it was already too late: Stephen Hricko was dead.

Kim, a hospital surgical assistant, told police that after the mystery party her husband had gotten drunk.

MURDER!

Join in the fun!!!???
Meet the suspects, victims & the persevering detective, with many local characters afoot!!
HELP SOLVE THE CRIME!!!???

Sat. April 9th, $35.00-7pm cocktails, 8pm   dinner w/wine
Sun. April 10th, $25.00-12:30 cocktails, 1:30 dinner

a gourmet meal with a cash bar
Avalon Theater, Easton
call for Reservations: Mark #820-0033

Other guests said Kim seemed especially absorbed in solving the staged murder case.

They had an argument, she said, and she went for a long drive to cool off. When she returned, she told them, she found the door locked and smoke pouring from the room.

There were problems with her story. Yes, there was a box of cigars near the bed, which might have played a role in the fire. But a toxicology test

DREAM ON: HE CLAIMED HE KILLED HIS WIFE WHILE SLEEPWALKING

Kim Hricko (under arrest, above) claimed that her husband, Stephen (below), died in a hotel room fire. Cops proved otherwise.

found no alcohol in Steve's blood. Even more telling: The tests showed that he had stopped breathing before the fire even began.

Police later learned that Kim had cooled on the marriage and might be having an affair, and that Stephen had refused to grant her a divorce. Most damning of all was the testimony of one of Kim's friends, who claimed Kim had revealed that she planned to kill her husband by injecting him with a drug that would stop his breathing and then setting fire to him. On Feb. 23 police arrived with an arrest warrant at a friend's house where Kim had taken refuge. She downed some 60 tablets of the anti-anxiety drug Xanax and threatened to kill herself with a razor, but officers quickly took her into custody.

"If she wanted a divorce," a friend of Stephen's later asked, "why didn't she just leave?" That part of the mystery was never solved.

THE VERDICT: Kim was convicted of first-degree murder and arson and sentenced to life in prison.

I T WAS A STUNNING MURDER—AND a bizarre defense. After dining at their Phoenix home around 7 p.m., Yarmila Falater asked her husband to fix the broken pump in their swimming pool. A 41-year-old engineer, Scott Falater went outside but quickly returned, saying, "It's too dark. I promise I'll be home tomorrow before it's dark and fix it then."

That night, around 9:30, he went to bed but rose shortly afterward, walked to his garage, changed into jeans and a T-shirt and picked up a hunting knife—perhaps to pry the seal off the defective pump. For reasons unknown, his wife joined him by the pool. For other reasons unknown—neighbors knew them as a friendly and loving couple—Scott stabbed Yarmila 44 times. All the while, the Falaters' two children slept peacefully upstairs. He then put the weapon and his bloody clothes in his Volvo—only to return and find that Yarmila, the only woman he had ever dated, was still breathing. A neighbor, alerted by her initial screams, peered over the backyard fence to see Scott standing over his wife. When Scott slipped on a pair of gloves, rolled Yarmila into the pool and held her head underwater, the neighbor bolted back into his house and phoned police. Officers arrived to find Scott, bloody but calm, coming down the stairs in his house.

His defense? Scott claimed he was sleepwalking, had no memory of the evening and no idea that he had killed his wife. He did, in fact, have a history of somnambulism: His mother later recalled that on four occasions when he was a teenager, he rose from bed, got dressed for school and came downstairs, only to be guided back to bed by his parents.

The jury wasn't buying. Expert witnesses stated that although it was true that sleepwalking afflicted roughly 9 percent of the population, the actions of a sleepwalker were decidedly unpredictable. By contrast, Scott's actions on the night of Jan. 16, 1997 had been carefully thought out: "Getting gloves, putting clothes in a container—what he did was not random," one expert said. "If he had really been doing it randomly, he would have killed his wife and then gone and planted some roses."

THE VERDICT: Found guilty of first-degree murder, Falater is currently serving a term of life without parole in Arizona.

Falater was still in his pajamas when he was booked.

"*The door opens, exposing the luxurious suite and Mr. and Mrs. Cromwell lying in bed. Their faces are of questioning horror as Hamilton closes the door gently . . . Zoom camera to [typing] paper; it reads, 'Five deaths to perfection—Chapter One: Mr. and Mrs. Jacob Cromwell.'*"

FROM A SCREENPLAY WRITTEN BY ERIK MENENDEZ

With famous friends and a Beverly Hills mansion, the Menendez family (from left: Lyle, Kitty, Jose and Erik) seemed to live the American dream.

FOLLOW THE MONEY

C ash. Bucks. Benjamins. Coin. Dinero, greenbacks, lucre, moolah. Bankroll, treasure, fortune, wad, beans, boodle, cabbage, dough. To that long list of synonyms for money might be added at least one more: motive. Next to love gone wrong, nothing stokes the homicidal urge like get-rich-quick.

Most startling of all? When greed trumps the bonds of marriage, family or romance. Raised in Beverly Hills, Lyle and Erik Menendez shot their parents, Jose and Kitty, 15 times with a shotgun, then blithely embarked on a luxe life of tennis lessons, hot cars and designer duds. Scam queen Sante Kimes, a frumpy 64-year-old who looked about as threatening as *Everybody Loves Raymond*'s Doris Roberts, left a trail of unwitting marks as she crisscrossed the country in search of easy money.

Like so many, Kimes dreamed of wealth but got three hots and a cot, in the slammer.

Lyle (left) said that after his father sexually abused him, he felt compelled to fondle his brother Erik.

BLOOD BROTHERS

It wasn't enough that their parents raised them in comfort. Lyle and Erik Menendez wanted it all—and were willing to kill for it

EAGER FOR SOME HIGH-SOCIETY GORE AND GLAMOR, THE boys had wanted to see the new Bond flick, *Licence to Kill.* The line was too long, so Lyle and Erik Menendez, 21 and 18, went to *Batman* instead. Afterward they dropped by a food festival in Santa Monica, then tried, but failed, to hook up for a late snack with a friend at a local Cheesecake Factory. Arriving home shortly before midnight Aug. 20, 1989, they were shocked, they later testified, to find the gate to their parents' Beverly Hills mansion unlocked. Even more unsettling, the front door was open.

Easing inside, they made their way to the den, where they came upon a horrifying sight: On the floor, next to a coffee table with half-eaten bowls of fresh berries and cream, lay their parents. Jose, 45, a Cuban-born entertainment executive who ran a prominent music-and-video distribution company and counted Barry Manilow and Kenny Rogers among his friends, had been pulverized by shotgun blasts, one to the head. His wife, Mary Louise, known as Kitty, 47, had been virtually ripped to bits with even more blasts. "I've never seen anything like it, never will see anything like it," Erik later told a reporter.

Given the violence of the slayings, police thought that Jose or his business might have run afoul of organized crime. They found a couple of tenuous connections between Jose's Live Entertainment and reputed mob figures, but

nothing convincing.

Meanwhile, the brothers, sole beneficiaries of their parents' estimated $14 million estate, went about reclaiming their lives—in grand fashion. Lyle dropped out of Princeton University and, using his share of an initial $400,000 insurance payout on his parents' deaths, bought a Porsche Carrera, a Rolex watch, designer threads and, with plans of starting his own business empire, a cafe that featured buffalo wings and was popular with Princeton students.

Erik, a graduate of Beverly Hills High, had even bigger plans: He hoped to fulfill his father's dream of becoming the first Cuban-American U.S. senator and to make Cuba a U.S. territory. "I'm not going to live my life for my father," he said, "but I think his dreams are what I want to achieve. I feel he's in me, pushing me." Before he got around to saving Cuba, though, he thought he'd try his luck as a professional tennis player and hired a full-time coach.

With a Beverly Hills mansion and lavish lifestyle, Jose and Kitty Menendez (above) seemed to pamper their two sons.

Mindful of the inheritance at stake, police kept an eye on the boys and began to glean bits of telling evidence. There was, for instance, the screenplay Erik had written in which an 18-year-old murders his parents for their money. Then a shotgun shell casing was discovered in a pocket of one of Lyle's jackets. In a highly unusual move, investigators subpoenaed tapes of Erik and Lyle speaking with their psychologist. Finally, on March 8, 1990, police made their move, arresting Lyle as he was leaving the family's home. Three days later Erik flew into Los Angeles from Israel, where he had competed in a tennis tournament, and turned himself in.

When the trial began in the summer of 1993, the prosecution's star witness, psychologist Jerome Oziel, told jurors that Erik had boasted to him that he and Lyle had committed the "perfect crime," killing "out of the hatred they had, in particular, for their father." The doctor was able to circumvent patient-client privilege because the brothers had threatened him as well.

It was seemingly damning testimony, and yet the case proved to be anything but open and shut. The brothers at first pleaded not guilty, then switched tactics. Yes, they said, they killed their parents—but in self-defense: Taking the stand, Lyle told a spellbound courtroom how his father had molested him sexually, beginning when he was just 6 or 7. Lyle also claimed his mother was abusive, rubbing his nose in the sheets when he had wet the bed and inviting him into her bedroom as she undressed. As he listened to his brother from the defense table, Erik wept. A confused jury could not reach agreement, and the judge declared a mistrial.

WHAT HAPPENED: On July 2, 1996, almost seven years after the murders, and after two hung juries and a retrial, Lyle and Erik were each sentenced to two terms of life without parole.

"She was going in and out of consciousness," said a woman who saw Lewis foaming at the mouth.

A Trip to Egypt, A Poisonous Snake

IT STARTED AS AN EXOTIC VACATION and ended tragically: Cheryl Lewis, 43, a British lawyer, lay on her bed in a Luxor, Egypt, hotel room, struggling to breathe. Neither her bereft boyfriend John Allan nor the doctors he summoned could figure out why. As the life ebbed out of Lewis, Allan curiously refused suggestions that he try to comfort her by telling her he loved her. Soon she was gone.

Months later Allan, 48, having returned to the Liverpool home he and Lewis had shared, reported her Mercedes missing. When it was found a few blocks away, police searched inside and found a bag packed with enough cyanide to kill more than 500 people. Before Allan was found guilty in March 2000 of poisoning Lewis and sentenced to life, the jury learned that he had been suspected of trying to kill two other women. He had also tampered with Lewis's will, making himself the beneficiary of her $690,000 estate.

"He doesn't seem to have a conscience," an officer said of John Allan (above).

Hunt recruited most of the members of the BBC from his exclusive L.A. prep school.

The Billionaire Boys Club Went for Broke

THEY CAME FROM RICH FAMILIES, BUT THE L.A. GROUP THAT came to be known as the Billionaire Boys Club burned through a *lot* of cash. Brought together by Joe Hunt, 27, when he formed the ad hoc investment fraternity in 1982, they were supposed to be savvy dealers in commodities and small businesses. They were better known for taking luxury ski trips, reckless gambling and collecting real estate. Freelance reporter Ronald Levin wondered where all that money came from and set a trap: He opened a brokerage account and asked Hunt to manage the money to see if Hunt dealt in legitimate investments. In truth, the account was phony. When Hunt learned in June 1984 that he had been duped and that Levin was investigating the BBC, he went ballistic—and Levin vanished. Before finding Hunt guilty of murder, jurors learned that the BBC had bilked investors out of millions. They also heard about a legal pad found in Hunt's home. On it, he had written, "At Levin's: TO DO," followed by instructions like "Tape mouth" and "Kill dog"—a seven-page recipe for murder. Hunt got life in prison.

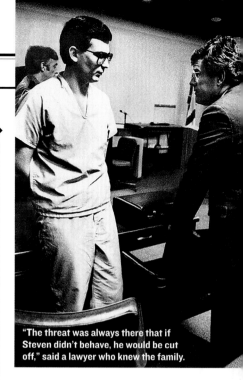

"The threat was always there that if Steven didn't behave, he would be cut off," said a lawyer who knew the family.

A CAR BOMB ON A QUIET MORNING

ON JULY 9, 1985, STEVEN BENson climbed into his mother's Chevy Suburban and went for coffee and doughnuts. The two weren't getting along. Margaret Hitchcock Benson, 63, heiress to a tobacco empire, was sick of Steven spending her money. The numbers weren't trivial: Steven, 34, a very unsuccessful businessman, had secretly written two checks totaling more than $100,000 on her account. Fed up, Margaret soon called her lawyer and told him to erase Steven from her will.

When Steven brought the truck back that day, he urged his mother,

Benson placed two pipe bombs in the truck: one between the front seats, the other hidden in the backseat.

Margaret began to fear that her son might want her dead so he could have her money.

sister and brother to take a ride. Moments after they climbed in, two pipe bombs ripped the truck apart. His sister was severely burned but miraculously was the only one to survive. Steven was convicted of homicide and is now serving life in prison.

Michelle Theer's boyfriend John Diamond (right) is serving life for murdering Marty Theer.

Catching A Two-Faced Killer

T IRED OF WAITING IN THE PARKING lot, Marty Theer, 31, an Air Force pilot, got out of his car and started up the steps to his wife's office. Seconds later he was thrown back by four shots from a 9-mm pistol. The triggerman? Former Army sharpshooter John Diamond—who had been having an affair with Theer's wife, Michelle, either 31 or 33 (she had two birth certificates), a Fayetteville, N.C., psychologist.

Diamond was convicted of murder, but Michelle, also a suspect, vanished. And stayed vanished for almost six months—until late 2002, when the police found her in South Florida. She had a new name and, thanks to plastic surgery, a new face. She too was charged with murder. The motive: Love—of money. Weary of Theer's military lifestyle, Michelle had hoped that his $500,000 life-insurance policy would pay the way to something grander. Instead she got life in prison.

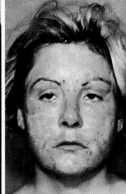

Michelle Theer, before (left) and after (right), had laser surgery on her face the day U.S. Marshals caught up with her. To his greedy wife's chagrin, Marty Theer (below) planned to be a military pilot.

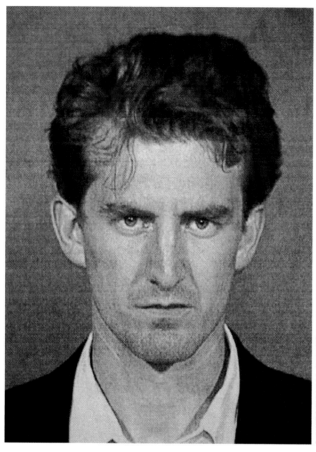
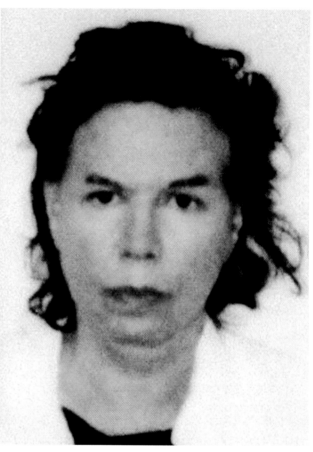

"We're not drifters or grifters," said Sante Kimes (right) after she and Kenneth were charged with murder. "We're just a mother and son."

TROUBLE IN APT. 1B

With the disappearance of a Manhattan landlady, the harrowing saga of two murderous mother-son scammers came to a close

PETITE BUT ENERGETIC, 82-YEAR-OLD IRENE SILVERMAN WAS A fastidious landlord. The luxury apartments in her six-story Manhattan townhouse, filled with art and antiques, attracted Wall Street moguls as well as such popular actors as Daniel Day-Lewis and Jennifer Grey. Silverman lived there herself; in fact she hadn't spent a night away from the building since 1986, 12 years before a prospective tenant named Manny Guerrin arrived at her door. In May 1998 Silverman had received a call from a woman claiming to be Guerrin's secretary. She explained that Guerrin was an important Mexican designer and that he needed an apartment in New York City. Silverman was surprised that Guerrin had no ID with him when he showed up, but the handsome young man did bring plenty of charm—and $6,000 in cash. Reluctantly, Silverman agreed to give Guerrin apartment 1B, as long as he filled out the application form the minute he had a chance.

He never turned in the paperwork. Moreover, she noticed that when he came and went from the building, he seemed to hide his face from the security cameras. Then she learned that he was secretly sharing the apartment with two other people. When Silverman pressed him to complete the application, Guerrin first said he would have to show it to his attorney, then quickly changed his tale to say that he had already submitted it to Silverman. "That's a lie," she said. That same day, Silverman showed a building maintenance man a sketch she had made of Guerrin, telling him, "This is for evidence."

When Silverman dined July 4 with friends, she assured them she was going to evict the troublesome tenant. The next day, she buzzed Aracelis Rivera, a building employee, to ask if she would take her boxer Georgie for a walk. Later, when Rivera tried to check in with Silverman, no one answered her phone. Rivera went to Silverman's apartment, but the door was locked. That afternoon, Rivera called another building employee, who summoned police.

That same day, July 5, police had a surprise of their own in store. They had received an unsolicited call from a Stanley Patterson, a thug who was up on gun charges for having sold weapons to a mother-son team suspected in a variety of scams in several states. He told police that he had just gotten a call from them, asking him to fly from Las Vegas to New York, where they wanted him to manage a fancy townhouse for them. When they all met at a Manhattan hotel, police were waiting, and pounced on Guerrin and his assistant. In truth, the two were Kenneth Kimes Jr., 23, and his mother, Sante, 64.

Before the day was out, police had a mountain of evidence implicating the Kimeses in a murder plot. Searching their car, their apartment and a hotel room they had booked, cops found guns and a date-rape drug for knocking someone unconscious, as well as Silverman's keys, Social Security card and blank checks. In a suitcase the pair had a bogus deed for Silverman's townhouse and notes that Sante Kimes had written to herself. One reminded her to "Get her signature some way," and a second wondered, "Who are her friends?"

Irene Silverman's apartment keys were found on Kenneth Kimes.

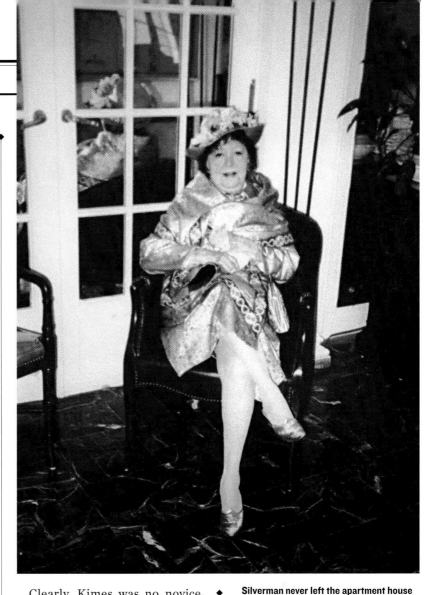

Silverman never left the apartment house without a friend or one of her employees.

Clearly, Kimes was no novice. Indeed the Oklahoma native's remarkable criminal odyssey began in 1961, when she was arrested for petty theft. In addition to a number of quick-money scams, she was arrested for enslaving servants in three different homes she kept with her late husband, Kenneth, a self-made construction company millionaire who, in willing his estate to her, was probably also a victim of her cunning. In more recent years, she and her son, who had joined in her crimes, were suspected in the disappearance of a banker, auto theft, arson, insurance fraud and the murder of David Kazdin, an associate of theirs who was found shot to death in a trash bin near Los Angeles International Airport. "Sante Kimes is probably one of the greatest cons who ever lived," said retired FBI agent Tom Nicodemus. "She could present this totally innocent front and then turn right around and stab you in the back."

Silverman's body was never found, but the Kimeses were charged with second-degree murder, robbery, forgery and other crimes, all as part of a scheme to bilk her out of her $7 million mansion. "They murdered her to get her out of the way," said the prosecutor. "It's as simple as that."

THE VERDICT: On May 18, 2000, the two were convicted of more than 100 charges and sentenced to at least 120 years—each. When the Kazdin murder case came to court, Kenneth, hoping to avoid the death penalty, ratted out his mother, finally breaking her spell on him.

Daniel Pelosi caused a stir when he arrived at a bar in Manhattan in August 2003 with a box containing Generosa's ashes. He ordered a beer for himself and a cosmo for her. "I was fulfilling her wishes," he said.

SHOCKING: THE ELECTRICIAN DID IT

THE BLUDGEONED NUDE BODY OF FINANCIER TED Ammon, 52, was found in his palatial East Hampton home on Oct. 22, 2001—just days before the divorce from his estranged wife, Generosa, was finalized. Chance? Not likely. The timing meant that Generosa, 45, could keep his entire $46 million estate—and that fact got police to thinking. They quickly learned that she was canoodling with Daniel Pelosi, 35, the electrician who had installed the property's security system. She and

Pelosi wed not long afterward, though clearly she came to have issues with him. When she died of cancer, she left conflicting wills, one that virtually cut out an enraged Pelosi. Nothing upset him quite as much, however, as when an old flame testified in his 2004 trial on charges that he had conspired with Generosa to kill Ammon. The woman recalled that Pelosi confessed to her, "I bashed his f---ing brains in, and he cried like a bitch . . ." Pelosi is serving a term of 25 years to life for second-degree murder.

A friend said she thought Ammon and Generosa (with their twins) had once been "happy as clams."

"There ain't no goddamn case against me," Pelosi (with Generosa) said of the investigation into Ammon's murder.

Dead Man's Hand

◆ Binion's murder, said a district attorney assigned to the case, "has it all. It involves drugs, sex, greed and violence."

I
N THE WEE HOURS OF SEPT. 19, 1998, County Sheriff's Sgt. Ed Howard was cruising through Pahrump, Nev., when he witnessed a most curious sight. Three men using an excavator were digging a trench in an empty lot. Even more puzzling, a quick search of a nearby truck revealed a mountainous cache of silver coins and bars. The sergeant promptly arrested the men—with good reason, as it turned out. The silver belonged to Ted Binion, 55, the troubled owner of the Las Vegas Horseshoe Casino, who had suspiciously died of a drug overdose two days before.

From the beginning, Benny Binion had intended that his son Ted inherit his downtown casino. As his sister Becky Behnen always said, Ted "was good with people and with numbers. The casino business was made for him." But in the ◆ late 1970s, after Ted had taken over, he developed an abiding affection for drugs. He became so addicted to heroin that he couldn't stop even after an overdose killed his sister Barbara in 1983. Four years later the state gaming commission suspended his license.

He never did get the license back, and after his mother died in 1994 and his wife and daughter ran off the next year, Binion hit bottom. That's about the time he took up with Sandy Murphy, 23, a topless dancer. She might have satisfied him on some levels, but he wasn't crazy about how she ran up huge bills on his credit cards. He didn't know it at the time, but she was also getting cozy with Rick Tabish, a friend of Binion's who owned a trucking business. Also worth noting perhaps: Tabish was $500,000 in the hole to ◆ the IRS and a local bank.

When Ted lost his license and Becky took over the Horseshoe, he arranged to retrieve the $5 million stash of silver bars and rare coins he had stored in the casino safe. He planned to move it to an underground vault he had in Pahrump, and called his buddy Tabish to handle the details. At about the same time, on Sept. 16, after yet another spat with Murphy, Binion phoned his lawyer and told him, "Take Sandy out of the will if she doesn't kill me tonight. If I am dead, you will know what happened."

Murphy called 911 the next afternoon to report that Binion had "stopped breathing." Given the paraphernalia and empty bottle of sedatives near Ted's body, police assumed he had OD'd. The tale might have ended there if Sergeant Howard hadn't spotted that excavator two nights later. Tabish was one of the three men arrested and though he was quickly released on bail, both he and Murphy were charged nine months later with murder.

WHAT HAPPENED: In 2000 they were both found guilty. But an appellate judge found insufficient evidence and granted them a new trial. In 2003 they were acquitted of murder and convict-
◆ ed on charges of larceny and burglary.

When he was deeply intoxicated, Binion sometimes asked his trusted friend Tabish (above) to look after his girlfriend Murphy (right).

The O.J. Simpson case had "love, lust, lies, hate, fame, wealth, beauty, obsession, spousal abuse, stalking . . . the bloodiest of bloody knife-slashing homicides, and all the justice money can buy."

FROM *JUSTICE* BY DOMINICK DUNNE

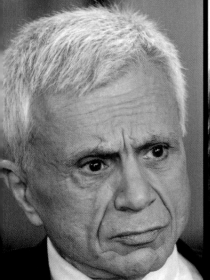

HOLLYWOOD & CRIME

We love celebrity. We love crime. Combine the two, add 24-hour cable news, *Access Hollywood, Entertainment Tonight* and E!, bake for nine months (the length of the O.J. trial) on Court TV and sprinkle lightly with Jay Leno's monologue—and you have the recipe for a cultural perfect storm.

The law, of course, tries to treat all defendants equally. Not so the press: Martha Stewart's trial would have been a blip on the business page—at *most*—if she had been some drab-gray corporate anonymouse. Still, in court, celebrities *are* different from you and me: They have (O.J. lawyer) Johnnie Cochran or (William Kennedy Smith lawyer) Roy Black—both of whom helped persuade juries to find their clients not guilty.

The saddest cases? When the celebrity at the heart of the story—like Tejana singer Selena or stalked Hollywood starlet Rebecca Schaeffer—is simply the innocent victim. ■

THE MANY TRIALS

An acquaintance of Nicole Simpson's claimed that O.J. once confronted her, saying, "If I can't have you, I'll kill you."

OF O.J.

The white Ford Bronco. The Bruno Magli footprint. The bloodstained gloves. In the end, they weren't enough. O.J. walked, but an obsessed public has continued to pass judgment on a once-revered football legend

THAT MORNING, O.J. SIMPSON played golf with a friend. In the afternoon, he and his former wife Nicole Simpson attended a performance at their daughter's school, though they didn't sit together. Afterward Nicole went with friends to a Brentwood, Calif., restaurant, where her mother accidentally left a pair of glasses. Ronald Goldman, 25, a waiter at the restaurant who had befriended Nicole, volunteered to take the glasses to her and clocked out at 9:30 p.m. Across town at 11:45 p.m., O.J., off on a business trip, boarded a flight to Chicago. **THE CRIME:** Around 10:30 or 11 that night—Sunday, June 12, 1994—Nicole's neighbors heard dogs barking frantically. Responding to a 911 call, police stepped into a horrific crime scene: Nicole, 35, lay dead on the walkway to her condo, her face bruised and throat slashed; Goldman, stabbed to death, lay in the bushes nearby.

Police reached O.J. by phone shortly after he checked into a Chicago hotel at 4:15 a.m., and he rushed back to L.A. The former football hero claimed he was devastated, but police already considered him a suspect. Their interest escalated exponen-

'It could be he's headed right back here to turn himself in,' said one police officer watching the Bronco chase. 'Yeah,' answered another, 'or else he's going to blow his brains out'

Goldman, who sometimes drove Nicole's car, told a friend that if O.J. ever caught him behind the wheel "He'd kick my butt."

tially four days later when cops spotted the now-notorious white Ford Bronco driven by O.J.'s close friend Al Cowlings. Inside, O.J., holding a gun, seemed despondent, as if he were considering taking his life. As cops—who at first thought he might be headed to Mexico—followed closely behind, reporters in helicopters broadcast live images of the bizarre motorcade, which eventually came to a halt at O.J.'s Los Angeles estate.

So began, if not the Crime of the Century, certainly the Celebrity Media Trial Extravaganza of the Century. The man at the heart of the story, O.J. Simpson, 47, was an American idol—gridiron star, successful actor, famous rental-car pitchman, a rare celebrity who always took time to sign autographs. His popularity fed disbelief and curiosity, and the public hungered, it seemed, for every scrap of information. Judge Lance Ito made a fateful decision: He would allow

cameras in the courtroom, making Ito, in effect, the producer of a daily celebrity soap opera—where the stakes were life and death.

THE TRIAL: Like any good soap opera, it boasted quirky characters and surprising twists—everything but an Evil Twin. Prosecutor Marcia Clark was buttoned-up but intense. The defense team—with Robert Shapiro, Johnnie Cochran, F. Lee Bailey, Barry Scheck and Alan Dershowitz—was the most unrelenting offensive line the elusive running back had ever known. Few cops were more gung-ho than ex-Marine Mark Fuhrman, who found incriminating blood samples in O.J.'s car and a bloodstained glove on his estate.

The evidence against Simpson seemed daunting. The prosecution argued that O.J. had beaten Nicole before, citing among other things his 1989 plea of no contest to spousal abuse and a 1993 tape on which she had said, "When he gets this crazed,

Sometime-actor Brian "Kato" Kaelin, who lived in O.J.'s guesthouse, heard strange sounds the night of the murders.

the legal system to the prosecution's presentation, Ito's handling of the case and the abilities of the jurors.

THE SECOND ACT: Few were as incredulous at the verdict as Ron Goldman's family. In their civil suit, a jury found in 1997 that the evidence did implicate O.J. and ordered him to pay $33.5 million in damages.

Bookstores virtually had to dedicate a new section to O.J.-related volumes, as most of the key players in the drama, even Fuhrman, published their accounts of the case and enjoyed hefty paydays.

O.J., who moved to Miami, maintains his innocence. He has managed to shield his assets and has barely paid a penny of the judgments. He plays golf often and, in a 2004 interview on the *Today* show, said that he has never spoken to his children, Sydney, now 19, and Justin, 16, about their mother's murder: "When the kids are ready to talk about it, they'll talk about it," he said. "Thus far they haven't."

I get scared." Claims were made that O.J. wanted Nicole back and was furious that she may have taken Goldman as her lover. The distinctive print of a size-12 Bruno Magli shoe was found at the scene. Simpson wore a 12 but famously claimed he would never wear such "ugly-ass shoes." (After the trial, photos surfaced showing Simpson wearing Bruno Magli shoes prior to the date of the murders.)

Still, the prosecution had problems. Fuhrman's testimony was tainted when the defense revealed a bigoted remark he had made, suggesting, they said, he might have issues with a black defendant. Memorably, the prosecution asked O.J. to try on the incriminating bloody gloves—and, at least the way he tugged at them, they seemed too small.

THE VERDICT: When the state rested, after nearly 250 days of trial, the massive press corps retired to their tents for what they thought would be a long wait. Instead, the jury deliberated

just four hours. The verdict—"Not guilty"—stunned most trial watchers; even O.J. nearly collapsed when he heard the words. Pundits leaped in, second-guessing everything from

O.J. said the bloodstained gloves were too small. Lawyer Johnnie Cochrane famously told the jury, "If the gloves don't fit, you must acquit."

A WINTER NIGHT, A SHOT RANG OUT

HER FOUR YEARS WITH SKI GREAT SPIDER SABICH "WERE THE HAPPIEST and richest of my life," waiflike singer Claudine Longet said. "We probably were everything that a man and woman should be to each other. He was my best friend." But when Longet, 35, called police to the home they shared near Aspen, Colo., one evening in March 1976, Sabich, 31, lay dead from a single shot from a .22-cal. pistol. Longet, whose three children from her 13-year marriage to crooner Andy Williams also lived in Sabich's handbuilt stone-and-timber house, told police that the gun had accidentally gone off as the World Pro ski champ tried and apparently failed to show her how to safely handle the weapon. A ballistics expert would say that the gun's safety was defective and friends and family, including Williams, rallied round, but disbelieving locals displayed IT'S ALL CLAUDINE'S FAULT bumper stickers. And the then-new NBC comedy show *Saturday Night Live* aired a famously outrageous bit in which Chevy Chase's TV sports announcer exclaims when shots ring out during a skiing competition "He's been accidentally shot by Claudine Longet!" Tried for felony manslaughter, Longet was convicted of criminally negligent homicide, a misdemeanor. She received a 30-day jail sentence.

A Louse in the House of Gucci?

"Maurizio and I were the most beautiful couple in the world," Reggiani (in '95) said. But "it all went wrong."

Benedetto Ceraulo, a petty criminal, was ultimately hired to do the hit.

IMPECCABLY DRESSED TO THE messy end, Maurizio Gucci—wearing a suit and tie and, of course, Gucci loafers—was on his way to work in the Milan headquarters of the family business when an unidentified man shot him twice in the back. In a gruesome flourish, his assailant added insult to lethal injury by shooting him once more in the face. Police did not have to look far for likely suspects. Ousted in Maurizio's ruthless 1984 takeover of the leather and luxury goods company founded by his grandfather were his three cousins and fellow heirs, as well as their father. "From a humanitarian point of view, I am sorry," said his ex-wife Patrizia Reggiani, the mother of Maurizio's two daughters, upon learning of his death. "But I can't say the same is true on a personal level."

Three years later Reggiani herself was on trial for the murder, accused of paying a friend $300,000 to rub out her ex, who had, she said, stiffed her on their alimony agreement, often paying only $90,000 per month instead of the stipulated $150,000. "He gave me the bones, but not the chicken," she said, adding during her

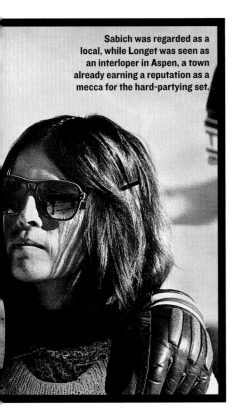

Sabich was regarded as a local, while Longet was seen as an interloper in Aspen, a town already earning a reputation as a mecca for the hard-partying set.

"He was trapped in a marriage he wanted no part of," a cop said of Blake (in 2000).

COPS & ROBERT: BLAKE GOES FREE

I N THE PILOT EPISODE OF ROBERT BLAKE'S HIT '70S SERIES BARETTA, THE title character's fiancée is murdered in front of an Italian restaurant. More than 25 years later, the veteran actor's real-life wife, Bonny Bakley, was shot to death in front of an Italian restaurant—and this time Blake, then 67, became the prime suspect. At his trial both sides cited his loveless marriage to Bakley, 44, a grifter who allegedly had run a lonely-hearts mail swindle at one point. Blake had married Bakley after learning that he was the father of her daughter Rose, whom he grew to dote upon. Even though she stayed in a cottage on his property, they never lived together as husband and wife. Blake hired private eyes to investigate her background and allegedly tried to get her arrested.

Prosecutors saw plenty of motive: "This was a hit by a husband," one police captain said just after Blake's arrest. The defense maintained that there was no physical evidence linking Blake to the shooting and that the prosecution's key witnesses, two stuntmen, were not credible. Blake hoped, as Baretta used to say, jurors would "take dat to da bank." They did, acquitting him of murder in March 2005. (Like O.J., he still faces a civil suit.)

Bakley (in 1986) had allegedly used provocative photos to tempt lonely men.

testimony that she often said she'd like to see him dead but was shocked that anyone would take her seriously. In 1998 she was convicted and sentenced to 26 years in prison.

'She was extremely curious and spirited. She managed to become successful and remain unjaded'

—EX-BOYFRIEND SEAN SIX

THE STALKER: FAME'S DARK SHADOW

Young and full of promise, actress Rebecca Schaeffer died when she greeted a stranger

ALTHOUGH SHE NEVER GOT A CHANCE TO TRULY SHINE, REBECCA SCHAEFFER WAS OFF TO a great start in Hollywood. "I took one look and fell in love with her," recalled a Portland, Ore., talent agent who met her early on. "She had a fresh charismatic way about her and was very gorgeous, with big brown eyes, dimples and a beautiful smile." In L.A. she landed a costarring role in the 1986 CBS series *My Sister Sam,* with Pam Dawber of *Mork & Mindy* fame, and a part in the film comedy *Scenes from the Class Struggle in Beverly Hills.* Even as her career began to take off, she remained, a friend said, the same "talented, beautiful-faced girl who worked extremely hard and was very nice." Robert John Bardo, a disturbed 19-year-old Tucson resident police described as an obsessive fan, showed up at her door one summer morning in 1989. The 21-year-old actress's neighbors later recalled seeing Bardo, a furtive stranger in a yellow polo shirt who approached them carrying a glossy publicity still of Schaeffer, asking where she lived. "You think about it for a second and then go your own way," said a woman who saw him twice. "That's what you do in L.A."

The intercom in her apartment was on the fritz, so that morning Schaeffer answered the door in person. No one knows if anything was said. Neighbors reported hearing a single shot and two screams. "It was bloodcurdling," said one. Another went to her aid, only to find Schaeffer lying in her doorway, dead from a single shot to the chest. The stranger in the yellow shirt was seen jogging down the street. The next day police, acting on a tip from a friend whom Bardo had told of his obsession, arrested him in Tucson.

Schaeffer's death became emblematic of every celebrity's worst fear: the random, psychotic fan who appears without warning, holding a gun. Nearly nine years before Schaeffer's murder, John Lennon was shot in the back by a so-called fan whose act seemed madness to most but made sense to John Hinckley Jr., who was said to have been partly inspired in his attempted assassination of Ronald Reagan a few months later. Michael J. Fox, David Letterman, Brooke Shields, Michael Douglas, Madonna, ice-skater Katarina Witt and Steven Spielberg are just a few of the famous who have been targeted by obsessive fans (Spielberg's was caught carrying handcuffs, razor blades, a boxcutter, duct tape, photos of Spielberg and a list of his family members). Said a Los Angeles security expert at the time of Schaeffer's killing: "It's getting much worse . . . ◆

because of the emphasis on the personal lives of media figures, particularly on television. Nowhere in history could you completely 'know' someone like you can now 'know' Johnny Carson."

STALKER'S FATE: Bardo was found guilty of murder in '91 and sentenced to life in prison.

An unemployed janitor, Bardo wrote Schaeffer a love letter, then threatened to harm her.

No one "who really knew her would do this," said *Scenes* director Paul Bartel.

TERRORIST OR TERRORIZED?

T WO MONTHS AFTER SHE WAS DRAGGED SCREAMING FROM her home and stuffed in the trunk of a car by masked, gun-toting kidnappers, Patty Hearst's voice was heard in a taped statement in which she declared her intention to "stay and fight" side by side with her tormentors in the Symbionese Liberation Army. Accompanying the tape sent to news outlets in April 1974 was a color photo of Hearst, 19-year-old granddaughter of millionaire press magnate William Randolph Hearst, dressed as an urban guerrilla and holding a submachine gun while standing in front of a flag bearing the seven-headed cobra symbol of the SLA. Later that month Hearst was seen in an even more shocking pose—as an armed accomplice in a San Francisco bank robbery, in which members of the SLA heisted $10,960. Pictures from

security cameras showed her brandishing an automatic weapon. Hearst "absolutely was a participant," said a bank guard. "She wasn't scared, I'll tell you that. She had a gun and looked ready to use it."

After surviving a shootout with police at a Los Angeles safe house (the leader of the SLA, an escaped convict who anointed himself Field Marshall Cinque, and five followers were killed; Hearst and other SLA members watched it on television from a nearby motel room), Tania, as the heiress called herself, spent 16 months underground before her arrest in San Francisco in September 1975. Despite psychiatric evaluations that supported her defenders' claim that Hearst was the victim of traumatic stress and coercive torture, she was deemed competent and ordered to stand trial.

Public opinion was sharply divided between those who branded her a terrorist and others swayed by press reports detailing her sufferings—locked in a closet for days at a time, she had been bound, raped and threatened with death—but the jury was not. Convicted of bank robbery and sentenced to seven years in federal prison, Hearst served 22½ months before then-President Jimmy Carter commuted her term in 1979. In 2001 she was granted a full pardon by President Clinton. "I had five years taken out of my life, either as a kidnap victim or a prisoner," said Hearst, who dropped the appeal of her sentence in 1982. "I realized it would take years to clear my name. My life had to go in another direction."

UPDATE: Now 51, Hearst raised two daughters with her husband and former bodyguard, Bernard Shaw. Her 1982 bestseller *Every Secret Thing* chronicles her ordeals.

Max Factor Heir's Date with Destiny

"CAN I TOUCH YOUR CHEST?" With pickup lines like that, Andrew Luster must not have had much luck on the dating scene. Which may begin to explain why the burly millionaire heir to the Max Factor cosmetics fortune resorted to far more boorish— and violent—behavior. In the summer of 2000, Luster was arrested in California after a woman told police that he had drugged her at a Santa Barbara bar, then taken her to his home, where he raped her. Unknown to her, his bedroom was rigged with hidden cameras that allowed Luster to videotape and photograph himself having sex with unconscious women. The not-quite-Mensa-level thought process that led him to preserve irrefutable evidence of his own wrongdoing? By filming his victims, whom he rendered unconscious by dosing them with gamma hydroxybutyrate (GHB), an illegal narcotic, Luster reasoned, they would never go to the police because the photos and tapes would make each victim, he later said, "look like a fool."

Which proved a spot-on description of Luster himself. The surfer and would-be playboy was charged with 86 counts of rape, sodomy, poisoning and other crimes after three of his victims did indeed go to police. Free on $1 million bail posted by his family, Luster was confined to his Ventura County home during the trial. Sensing things weren't going his way—the jury didn't appear to be buying his contention that he was an aspiring porn director—Luster went on the lam, fleeing his home in January 2003. Six months later the fugitive was collared by bounty hunter Duane Lee "Dog" Chapman in Puerto Vallarta, Mexico, as he was about to enjoy a predawn beef taco at a roadside stand. Chapman, who was arrested for his efforts—bounty hunting is illegal in Mexico—said he had received a tip from an American couple who had seen a news report about Luster and recognized him as an American they'd met on vacation in Mexico.

Bundled into a van and quickly repatriated to the U.S., the 39-year-old Luster was apparently so confident of his skills as a fugitive that he hadn't bothered to change his appearance other than to grow sideburns and a goatee. "You gotta be dumb to rape someone and videotape it," said a former surfing buddy, "but you've got to be even dumber to become a fugitive and hang out in Puerto Vallarta, the most popular west coast destination for Americans in Mexico. What an idiot."

THE VERDICT: Found guilty on all 86 counts, he was sentenced to 124 years in prison.

◆ **After Luster's capture (in L.A. in 2003), reporters found his diary (below), in which he jotted Spanish translations of clumsy come-ons like, "I will make you feel better."**

Sentenced to four years in prison for tax fraud in 1989, Leona served 18 months in a federal lockup. Charges were dropped against Harry due to mental incompetence.

For the Love of Money

L EONA AND HARRY HELMSLEY'S FLAGSHIP HOTEL IN NEW YORK CITY was billed as "the only palace in the world where the queen stands guard." According to federal authorities who charged the Helmsleys with tax fraud in 1988, the queen and her king had also bilked the U.S. Treasury to the tune of $4 million. Wealthy as they were, money was something that Leona, a 67-year-old, Brooklyn-born milliner's daughter, and Harry, a self-made billionaire who owned, among other properties, the Empire State Building, couldn't get enough of. Among their transgressions: listing as business expenses such improbable items as a $130,000 home stereo system, a $45,000 clock Leona gave Harry as a birthday present and $500,000 worth of jade that decorated their sprawling Connecticut mansion.

Some friends, and even family, were not surprised. Jay Panzirer, Leona's only child (from a previous marriage), died suddenly of a heart attack at age 40, leaving a $200,000 estate to his wife, Mimi, and four children. Leona and Harry, said Mimi, sued the estate for everything from back debts to the cost of shipping her son's body to New York. The grandchildren inherited $432 each. "She wiped me out," Mimi said. "To this day I don't know why they did it."

A FAMILY TORN APART: WOODY, MIA AND SOON-YI

MY ONE PUBLIC APPEARANCE IN years," Woody Allen lamented, "and all straight lines." So ended a difficult press conference where Allen admitted that yes, as his long-time lover Mia Farrow had claimed, he was involved in an on-going sexual relationship with one of her adopted children, Soon-Yi Previn, 21. Allen, 56, furiously denied Farrow's other charge: that he had molested daughter Dylan 7, whom they had adopted together. The usually press-shy director had also

The accuser was neither "a nut or a slut," as lawyers for Smith (in 1991) characterized her, said a Georgetown law professor.

"My children have been ripped apart emotionally," said Farrow (in happier times with baby Satchel, Dylan and Allen in 1988).

"It's a tragedy for the children that I was not awarded custody," Allen said.

Yi, moved quickly from the tabloids to a New York State courtroom. In a damning decision that Allen didn't even try to milk for a laugh, the judge dismissed his custody claims, scolding the actor for pursuing a relationship with Soon-Yi regardless of their family ties, for his "grossly inappropriate" behavior toward Dylan and for being an inattentive parent who didn't know the names of the kids' dentist, their friends or their pets. The closest to a laugh line was delivered by the judge, who said Farrow's principal shortcoming as a parent "appears to have been her continued relationship with Mr. Allen."

UPDATE: Soon-Yi and Allen, who reportedly has no contact with his sons and daughter with Farrow, wed in 1997. They have two daughters of their own.

announced that he was suing for custody of Dylan, Moses, 14, and Satchel, 4. The couple's battles, which became public in 1992, after Farrow discovered a stack of nude Polaroids Allen had taken of Soon-

A Kennedy on Trial—On TV

A COURTROOM DRAMA FOLLOWED BY MILLIONS, THE WILLIAM KENNEDY Smith rape trial was a riveting spectacle set on Florida's glamorous Gold Coast in Palm Beach County. The televised trial even featured a memorable special effect—a blue dot superimposed over the accuser's face to preserve her anonymity. The male lead, Smith, was a good-looking 31-year-old med-school grad and rich kid from one of the nation's most illustrious families. His accuser was an unnamed mystery woman cast by the prosecution as a wronged innocent and by defense lawyers as a sexual predator and femme fatale. From their front-row seats, jurors had to choose between two opposing story lines. According to Smith, the woman picked him up at Au Bar, a struggling Palm Beach nightclub rescued from oblivion by the case's notoriety, and drove him home to the storied oceanfront Kennedy compound, where they had consensual sex. According to his accuser, the two were walking on the beach when Smith suddenly jumped out of his clothes and into the ocean. When she didn't join him, he ran out of the water, tackled her and raped her. "I thought he was going to kill me," she testified.

Smith's mother, Jean, as well as JFK Jr., was among Smith's supporting cast.

THE VERDICT: In December 1991, after less than 90 minutes of deliberation, the jury acquitted Smith of the charges.

THE FALL AND FALL OF MICHAEL JACKSON

As Pop's Peter Pan slid into surreal self-parody, child molestation charges blighted the memory of a once-brilliant career

I N THE OFTEN-LURID ANNALS OF AMERICAN celebrity—even within his famously dysfunctional family—the arc of Michael Jackson's life has no parallel. Child star, to icon, to sideshow eccentric, to accused pedophile—who at the very least admitted he'd happily bedded down with other people's little boys. It was a long, strange train wreck mapped in his eerily evolving appearance. Circa 1970 the boy soprano beamed under an Afro. Lithe and silky in the '80s, he bobbed his nose and acquired an almost feminine beauty. "Moonwalking" in white glove, moussed locks and black fedora, the self-styled King of Pop inhaled Grammys, amassed $200 million and seemed invincible. Come the 1990s, cosmetic surgery squared his jaw and reduced his nose to an elfin nub. His albums were no longer blockbusters and debts drained his fortune. Jackson's vast arsenal of idiosyncrasies fed a generation of stand-up comedians. Enter the age of Wacko Jacko.

And then there were the boys. For years Jackson had portrayed himself as the eternal child, like his hero Peter Pan—fey, innocent, asexual. A disproportionate number of his friends were preadolescent males. Some were famous—including child actors Emmanuel Lewis and Macaulay Culkin—but most were obscure. Many slept over at the 2,700-acre ranch and theme park near Santa Barbara he calls Neverland. "I don't think you could suggest to Michael Jackson that he shouldn't be around children," said his onetime attorney Bertram Fields. "He loves children."

The question was: "How?" To child abuse experts, Jackson raised more red flags than Lenin. "People like me go, 'What is going on with this guy?'" says clinical social worker Joan Johnson of UCLA Medical Center. Then, in the fall of 1993, the other high-top dropped: The 13-year-old son of a Beverly Hills dentist filed a multimillion-

In 2003 Jackson appeared in a documentary with the boy who later charged him with abuse.

dollar suit accusing Jackson of sexual battery and seduction. In the course of the investigation, the King of Pop was compelled to let police examine and photograph his genitalia, which the boy had described in meticulous detail. Giving America a little too much information, Jackson made an anguished pre-Christmas TV appearance and in a high, quavery voice vividly recounted the search—"the

most humiliating ordeal of my life," he called it, and who could blame him? The next month—ironically, at an NAACP Image Awards Dinner—he bucked up, proclaiming, "The truth will be my salvation."

Or, failing that, $15-to-$20 million—the amount he reportedly paid his accuser, who later dropped the suit. Jackson's attorneys, among them a pre-O.J. Johnnie Cochran, stressed the deal was no admission of guilt, noting that the fabulously rich, child-friendly superstar was an easy mark for extortion. Little did the public know that in 1994 Jackson made a second settlement, for $2.4 million, with the son of a former maid who accused the singer of fondling him.

Yet Jackson continued to consort with his favorite demographic, 8-to-13-year-old males, shopping, dining, going out on the town. At one point his handlers produced two boys who acknowledged they'd shared a bed

At his January 2004 arraignment, Jackson danced atop his SUV for an adoring throng—and incurred a judge's wrath.

with him but claimed, in the words of one youngster, that it was merely a harmless "slumber party." The point, apparently, was to portray Jackson as your average then-35-year-old kid. As spin, it was questionable at best. His endorsements dried up; notably, Pepsi cancelled a $10 million deal.

Even without the clouds of suspicion, Jackson's world was a work of surrealism on velvet (as if to stress the point, he even married Lisa Marie Presley). When he briefly wed a second time, to his dermatologist's assistant Debbie Rowe, both parties admitted the purpose was to produce his son Prince Michael I, now 8, and daughter Paris Michael, 7; Rowe, Jackson said, bore them "as a present" to him. In 2002 he welcomed a second son, Prince Michael II, borne, he says, by a surrogate mother. Jackson's parenting skills were called into question later that year when he entertained paparazzi by dangling the babe from a Berlin hotel balcony.

That was nothing compared to a controversial 2003 documentary about Jackson by British journalist Martin Bashir. In it, the singer is seen holding hands with a 12-year-old cancer survivor. At one point a wide-eyed Jackson says blithely, "I have slept in a bed with many children," the 12-year-old allegedly among them. He would live to regret that statement. The boy later claimed that Jackson had molested him, which led to police choppers and investigators swarming Neverland, and, eventually, a criminal trial by turns gripping and absurd. Jackson seemed to treat his January 2004 arraignment as a lark. He arrived 20 minutes late, angering judge Rodney S. Melville, who warned, "You have started out on the wrong foot with

In January an elegant and upbeat Jackson arrived for a pretrial hearing. "I will be acquitted and vindicated," he said.

me." After pleading not guilty, the accused danced on the roof of his SUV.

When the trial began a year later, it often seemed that Jackson still didn't get it. At times he'd arrive in one of his ornate quasi-military outfits— "like Captain Crunch," Chris Rock quipped—flashing victory signs, entourage in tow, including a large bodyguard whose job consisted of holding an umbrella over the boss's head. Once, reputedly roused from his sickbed, Jackson showed up in pajama pants (he hadn't had a chance to dress, he claimed, although he clearly did squeeze in time for pancake and eyeliner). As his floridly white-maned advocate Thomas

Mesereau Jr. clashed with D.A. Tom Sneddon, accusers past and present told harrowing tales of the singer's allegedly seducing boys with gifts and wine he called "Jesus Juice," of groping, kissing and other violations of the childhood innocence Michael Jackson so often professed to embody—and revere. "His people are telling him all the time, 'This is serious, Michael,'" said family friend Firpo Carr. "He pretty much thinks he can will this away. He's still in his own Neverland." Was it all an act? Where did reality and performance, guilt or innocence, begin and end? Did the Man in the Mirror even know anymore—or care?

MARV'S VERY PERSONAL FOUL

"I will have no more surprises," said Albert (in 1993) of the trial's revelations.

OOO! WAS THE FAN REACTION WHEN NBC'S VOICE OF PRO BASKET-ball, Marv Albert, whose trademark exclamation of triumph *Yesss!* is one of the most familiar in broadcast sports, was accused of a violent—and kinky—sexual attack on a longtime girlfriend. The woman claimed Albert had hurled her onto a bed in his Ritz-Carlton Hotel outside Washington, D.C., bit her repeatedly and forced her to perform oral sex. During a three-day trial, Albert suffered the further embarrassment of having his alleged sexual proclivities—a taste for hotel-room porn; threesomes, sometimes including male partners; and dressing in women's lingerie—aired in daily headlines.

To spare himself further humiliation—and also avoid a possible prison sentence of five years to life—Albert, then 56, pleaded guilty to a lesser charge of misdemeanor assault. NBC fired him that day. He received a one-year suspended sentence and was ordered to seek psychotherapy. But as Albert well knew, much can happen before the final buzzer. Less than two years after the trial, the *Yesss!* man was back in the NBC broadcast booth, where he resides still.

Hollywood Gothic: A Family Tragedy

As stipulated in the Hartmans' will, Sean and Birgen (in 1996) are being raised by Brynn's sister.

HEY ALWAYS SEEMED HAPPY," A FAVORITE BARtender recalled of regular customers Phil and Brynn Hartman. "They always held hands and laughed and seemed like they were having a good time." That image of the sunny Hollywood couple masked a deeply dysfunctional relationship between the outwardly charming, privately reserved comic actor and his wife of 10 years, who treated her own dire insecurities with a volatile mix of cocaine, alcohol and antidepressants. "She had to get amped up [on drugs] to get his attention, and when she got amped up, he would withdraw," a friend said of their frequent shouting matches. "And in the morning he'd wake up, and everything would be fine." After a heated argument on May 28, 1998, Brynn shot Hartman three times with a .38 handgun as he slept. She briefly fled but returned with a friend, who instantly called 911. When police arrived, they left Brynn in the bedroom as they escorted the couple's two children, Sean, 9, and Birgen, 6, to safety. In that moment, she shot herself in the head. "This is a tragedy beyond description," said Rita Wilson, Hartman's co-star in *Jingle All the Way.* "Now two children are left with a lifetime of confusion."

"I hate this process," she said after her sentencing. "It has been really devastating."

"She looks likes she's been to the Golden Door Spa," a pal said of Stewart (with employees, below, after her release from prison, above).

MARTHA IN THE BIG HOUSE

ISN'T IT NICE TO HAVE BROKERS WHO tell you those things?" Martha Stewart had just dumped 3,928 shares of ImClone Systems stock after receiving a tip, via her broker, from the company's CEO that the stock price was about to sink. As Stewart's fans had so often heard her proclaim, it seemed like "a good thing."

One day later the biotech company's value plummeted on news that the FDA had nixed ImClone's plans to market a once-ballyhooed new cancer drug. Stewart's sale saved her $45,000 in losses—but eventually cost her incalculably more. First, the timing raised eyebrows among execs at Merrill Lynch, where her broker Peter Bacanovic worked. Later, the U.S. Securities and Exchange Commission, the FBI and even Congress got involved. To head off accusations of insider trading, Stewart and Bacanovic, as well as his assistant Douglas Faneuil, claimed that they had a preexisting agreement to sell the stock if it ever slipped below $60 per share—

which it had the day of the sale.

Not so, Faneuil admitted later. He would become the star witness against Stewart, who in June 2003 was indicted for conspiracy, securities fraud and obstruction of justice. To many it seemed that Stewart had painted herself into a corner by not simply admitting wrongdoing. "Had she come forward and shot straight with us," said a spokesman for the congressional investigating committee, "this would have been over the next day." But lying to federal authorities and covering up the truth by doctoring phone records and dispensing gifts as hush money, as the prosecution alleged, was a recipe for disaster. "This case," said a prosecutor, "was all about lies."

In a six-week trial that began in January 2004, two years after the stock sale, it sometimes seemed that Stewart was on trial not for what she did but for who she was, an enormously successful woman whose often imperious ways— she called Faneuil an "idiot," according to

testimony, and once threatened to leave Merrill Lynch because she didn't like the music that played over the phone when she was put on hold—belied the sweet helpmate and homemaker she appeared to be on TV. "I think she is really struggling to maintain strength and carry on," her sister said after the verdict, adding that it was upsetting to witness "the glee that so many people seem to be having watching this happen."

UPDATE: Found guilty on four counts, Stewart served five months in Alderson Federal Prison Camp in rural West Virginia, where she endured the anemic thread counts in her bed linens and the hi-carb prison diet with aplomb. Her company's roller-coaster stock climbed steadily during her imprisonment and fell following her March 4, 2005, release.

RAPIST ON THE ROPES

Unlike Desiree Washington, ex-wife Robin Givens (in 1988) knew firsthand about Tyson's troubled history with women.

WEIGHING IN AT 108 LBS. AND PEPPERING HER SPEECH WITH teenspeak staples like "neat" and "yucky," 18-year-old Desiree Washington sounded young for her age. She certainly seemed no match for 250-lb. former World Heavyweight champ Mike Tyson, the brutally efficient boxer who was confident he would beat the charges of rape and criminal deviant conduct that she brought against him as handily as he disposed of opponents in the ring. "I'll win," he told a friend during his 13-day trial in 1992. "I always win."

Didn't happen. Washington testified that Tyson had slammed her onto a bed, pinned her with one massive forearm and raped her as she begged him to stop; the jury believed her and found him guilty on all counts. When his lawyer argued that Washington agreed to have sex because she was a gold digger attracted by his wealth and fame, her lawyer pointed to the petite, sniffling accuser, who had testified she was asleep when Tyson called on the night of the rape. "Being the wise and wily 18-year-old that she is," he said, "she puts on her jammies in her hotel room, goes to sleep and lies in wait for poor Mr. Tyson to call." Tyson served three years in prison. He never regained his boxing crown.

A Dark Vision— and a Darker Secret

ROMAN POLANSKI WAS A world-famous film director (*Rosemary's Baby*; *Chinatown*) with a tragic past: His mother died at Auschwitz; his wife, Sharon Tate, and four friends suffered horrible deaths at the hands of the Manson Family. His accuser was a 13-year-old schoolgirl. "I had a Spider-Man poster on the wall and I kept pet rats," she told PEOPLE many years later. Their worlds collided in 1977, when Polanski, 44, was accused of plying her with champagne and Quaaludes and luring her into a Jacuzzi for sex at the home of his pal Jack Nicholson, who was out of town at the time.

With Polanski awaiting trial, the case was debated in the media, with detractors casting the director as a demon sleaze from his own macabre film oeuvre and supporters spreading the word that he was trapped by a

"Life was hard for him, just like it was for me," his victim said of Polanski (in Santa Monica in '77).

worldly Lolita and her greedy mother. Polanski pleaded guilty to unlawful intercourse with a minor, then, rather than face sentencing, fled to Paris. He continues to produce award-winning films—including 2002's *The Pianist*—but cannot set foot in the U.S. without risking arrest and jail.

In 1997 his victim decided to speak publicly about the case for the first time. "If Polanski comes back, fine," she said. "That would at least end it. It will never be over until that happens."

Polanski "did something really gross to me," says Samantha Geimer (in 1976, left, and '97), now a married mom in Hawaii.

HE PRODUCED 45s—AND PACKED A .38

HANDCUFFED AND DAZED, PHIL Spector was in a world of pain. Arrested in February 2003, the diminutive record producer who had revolutionized '60s rock and roll was booked on suspicion of murdering 40-year-old B-movie actress Lana Clarkson. Her body was found in a pool of blood in the foyer of his turreted, castle-like home in Alhambra, Calif.

In his heyday Spector's "wall of sound" style had helped create classics like "To Know Him Is to Love Him" and "You've Lost That Lovin' Feelin'." But he hadn't had a big hit in almost a quarter century, and now he was known as much for reclusiveness and eccentricity—including a love for guns. Spector owned so many that he was known to coordinate his favorites with his wardrobe; he had brandished the weapons to frightening effect while working with John Lennon, the Ramones and ex-wife Ronnie Spector. In November 2003 police dismissed

Hours before his arrest (below), Spector picked up Clarkson (in '03) at her club.

Spector's claim that Clarkson, the statuesque star of 1985's *Barbarian Queen*, had shot herself, and charged him with murder. As this book went to press, he was out on bail and awaiting a trial in September 2005.

FROM FAN TO FANATIC: THE SAD DEATH OF SELENA

THEY COULD NOT HAVE BEEN more different. Vivacious, open-hearted and extravagantly talented, Tejana singer Selena Quintanilla-Pérez, 23, was a star. Plain-looking and guarded, Yolanda Saldívar was the 34-year-old former registered nurse who served as president of Selena's fan club and manager of the singer's lucrative boutique business. She had built a shrine to Selena in her home and worked tirelessly—and, initially, for free—on the singer's behalf. But while Selena

"She probably couldn't accept the fact that she wasn't going to be around Selena anymore," a coworker said of Saldívar (in '95).

once called Saldívar "my only friend," others were not so smitten with the enigmatic older woman. "She was mean; she was manipulative," said a designer who quit working for the singer's Selena Etc. fashion outlet because of conflicts with Saldívar. "I told Selena I was scared of Yolanda. She wouldn't let me talk to Selena anymore. She was very possessive."

At first Selena refused to believe scuttlebutt circulating among her entourage that Saldívar was ripping her off, embezzling thousands of dollars from her stores and siphoning funds from her fan club. Finally, in March 1995, the singer confronted her friend, who swore at first that she had documents that would prove her innocence. When Selena visited her room at a Corpus Christi, Texas, Days Inn on March 31, Saldívar said she didn't have the documents, which had been stolen, along with her car, in the Mexican border town of Laredo, where she claimed to have been raped. Concerned, Selena insisted she get medical attention. Once they were at the hospital, Saldívar admitted it was a lie; there were no docu-

ments. Returning to the motel, police said, Selena fired Saldívar and removed a $3,000 diamond-encrusted gold ring her friend had made for her. It was then, police said, that Saldívar produced a .38-cal. revolver she had purchased a few weeks before. A motel maid later said she saw Selena run from room 158 screaming "Help! Help!" After shouting "'You bitch!'" the maid said, "Yolanda shot her in the back."

As Selena lay mortally wounded on the floor of the Days Inn, she still gripped the ring in her hand. "I felt there was an obsession toward Selena, that she was unbalanced," her devastated father, Abraham Quintanilla Jr., said of Saldívar, who surrendered to police after a nine-hour standoff. "It's beyond me now. She has to answer to the Creator and the laws of the land."

THE VERDICT: Found guilty of first-degree murder in 1995 and sentenced to life, Saldívar, who is eligible for parole in 2025, is kept in protective isolation and given a three-person escort when moved within the prison.

Blue-collar kids who gave their all to excel, Harding and Kerrigan were friendly competitors (left, in 1994) until treachery laid Kerrigan low (below, in Detroit the same year).

Soulless on Ice: A Skater Is Attacked

A 1992 OLYMPIC BRONZE MEDAL WINNER, NANCY KERrigan was skating her way back from a so-so season when her dreams of competing in the '94 Games in Lillehammer, Norway, got whacked. After a practice round at the U.S. women's national figure-skating championships in Detroit, the deciding event for hopefuls vying to compete in Lillehammer, Kerrigan was catching her breath when a man approached her from behind and, without warning, struck her in the knee with what witnesses said was either a crowbar or a baseball bat. "Why? Why? It hurts so much," Kerrigan howled in pain as a crowd formed and the assailant disappeared. "Why me?" Coming as it did months after tennis star Monica Seles had been stabbed by a deranged fan of her rival, Steffi Graf, the attack sent shock waves beyond the rink. Fellow competitor Tonya Harding, 23, who two days later captured the championship that Kerrigan, 24, had been favored to win, was too frightened to sleep alone in her hotel room that night, her coach said later: "Tonya is really angry that the whole thing happened."

She had been angry, all right, but probably not because her erstwhile Olympic teammate had suffered a potentially career-ending injury. Harding's former bodyguard—who, along with her

Though she had twice sought restraining orders against Gillooly, Harding allegedly joined with him in the scheme.

ex-husband Jeff Gillooly, 26, and two others, was charged in the assault—later told a newspaper that the skater had been "pissed off and disappointed" that the attack had taken so long to carry out. Considering the source (the bodyguard had lied even to lead plotter Gillooly, telling him that Kerrigan had been struck half a dozen times, when in fact the assailant landed a single, off-center blow), many were willing to take Harding's word that she knew nothing about the scheme to knock her rival out of the competition. Within weeks, however, Gillooly—who had allegedly once threatened to have Harding's legs broken—also claimed that she had been involved in the sinister ice-capade from the beginning.

WHAT HAPPENED: Kerrigan recovered, went on to win the silver at Lillehammer and later joined the professional skating tour. Gillooly struck a deal and was sentenced to two years for his role in the attack. Harding competed at Lillehammer as well and her televised duel with Kerrigan drew more than 45 million U.S. households. As for the attack: In a plea bargain, Harding admitted to hindering investigators ("I'm really sorry that I interfered," she told the judge) and was given three years' probation. Stripped of her national championship and banned from professional skating by the U.S. Figure Skating Association, Harding gave up the world of double toe loops and, among other endeavors, tried to earn a few bucks, and pay off her legal fees, throwing uppercuts in women's boxing.

ROBERT DOWNEY JR. Nov. 25, 2000
Arrested for cocaine possession and being under the influence of drugs, Downey was sentenced to rehab and three years' probation.

LIL' KIM (AKA KIMBERLY JONES) July 24, 1996
The diminutive rapper was arrested for marijuana possession during a raid on the Teaneck, N.J., home of Notorious B.I.G. Police let her off with a warning.

EMINEM (AKA MARSHALL MATHERS)
June 2000 Charged in Michigan with carrying a concealed weapon and brandishing a weapon. He received a year of probation.

FAMOUS MUGS

In many a celebrity's life, there comes a day when they're *really* not ready for their close-up: The station-house portrait is just about the last head shot any star wants to take. The camera angles and lighting are seldom kind (except, perhaps, to the young Al Pacino; see page 105), and if you've landed the role, you can't pass it on to an understudy

BILL GATES Dec. 13, 1977
The future software billionaire was pulled over and arrested by Albuquerque police for a traffic violation.

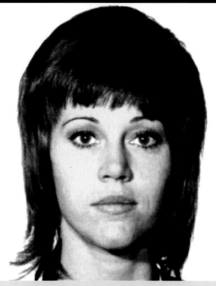

JANE FONDA Nov. 3, 1970
For allegedly kicking a police officer, Fonda was charged with assault and battery and released on $5,000 bond. Charges were eventually dropped.

NICK NOLTE Sept. 11, 2002
Charged with DUI for alcohol and other controlled substances, Nolte received three years' probation.

TIM ALLEN Oct. 2, 1978
Charged in Kalamazoo, Mich., with delivery of a controlled substance: cocaine. Allen served 28 months in prison.

BOBBY BROWN Nov. 7, 2002
Arrested in Atlanta for marijuana possession, speeding and driving without a license, Brown was tried for an outstanding warrant and given eight days in jail.

NICK CARTER March 5, 2005
The Backstreet Boy was pulled over in Huntington Beach, Calif., and charged, after failing a sobriety test, with driving while intoxicated.

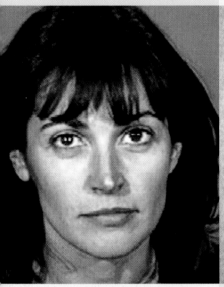

KIM DELANEY Jan. 26, 2002
After a citizen reported her driving erratically in Malibu, Delaney was arrested on suspicion of drunk driving.

MATTHEW MCCONAUGHEY Oct. 24, 1999
Police responded to a noise complaint at the actor's Austin home and found him playing bongos in the nude. They charged him with resisting arrest.

COREY FELDMAN March 9, 1990
Charged with possession of heroin and cocaine with intent to sell, the actor was sentenced to 10 months in rehab.

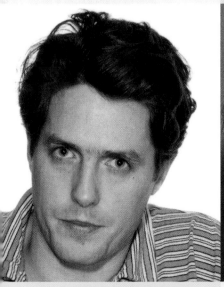

HUGH GRANT June 27, 1995
After being caught with a hooker in his car in L.A., Grant was charged with lewd conduct, fined $1,180, and put on probation.

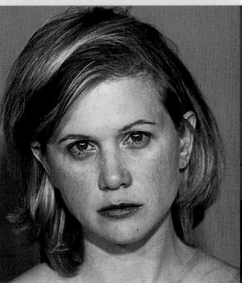

TRACEY GOLD Sept. 3, 2004
The *Growing Pains* star rolled her SUV with her husband and kids inside and pleaded guilty to a felony DUI charge in January 2005.

JACK WHITE Dec. 23, 2003
After beating up another Detroit rocker at a club, White was arrested, fined $500 and had to attend anger-management class.

EDWARD FURLONG Sept. 15, 2004
The animal-rights supporter was charged with public drunkenness after liberating live lobsters from a tank in a Kentucky supermarket.

R. KELLY Jan. 22, 2003
The singer was arrested on child-porn charges in Miami while already awaiting trial on 21 counts of child porn in Illinois due to an incriminating sex video.

GLEN CAMPBELL Nov. 24, 2003
Charged with drunk driving and hit-and-run after fleeing a fender-bender, the singer was released on $2,000 bail.

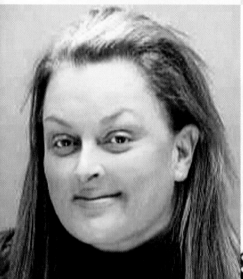

WYNONNA JUDD Nov. 13, 2003
Busted for drunk driving in Nashville, Judd posted $500 bond and made a public apology.

LARRY KING Dec. 20, 1971
King was charged with grand larceny for allegedly swindling a business partner. The case was dropped due to the statute of limitations.

KID ROCK Feb. 16, 2005
Rock was booked into custody by Nashville police after allegedly punching a disc jockey at a strip club.

JAMES BROWN Jan. 28, 2004
At 71, Brown allegedly beat wife Tommie Rae, 35, and threatened her with a chair. He pleaded no contest to domestic violence charges.

MACAULAY CULKIN Sept. 17, 2004
Arrested for possession of marijuana and a controlled substance—16 sleeping pills and eight Xanax—the actor was briefly jailed before posting $4,000 bond.

VINCE VAUGHN April 12, 2001
The actor got into a bar brawl while filming in Wilmington, N.C. The fighting-in-public charges were later dropped.

TOMMY LEE Dec. 10, 1997
Mötley Crüe's bad-boy drummer was arrested after allegedly knocking over a security guard at a concert in Phoenix.

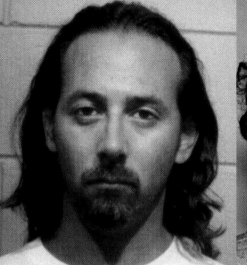

PEE-WEE HERMAN (AKA PAUL REUBENS)
July 26, 1991 Charged with indecent exposure, Reubens was fined $50, given 75 hours of community service and had to produce an antidrug video.

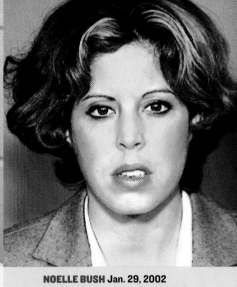

NOELLE BUSH Jan. 29, 2002
President Bush's niece was charged with using a fake prescription to buy Xanax. She was ordered to do a 16-month stint in rehab.

DUDLEY MOORE March 21, 1994
The actor was arrested after allegedly beating future wife Nicole Rothschild. She refused to press charges.

SCOTTIE PIPPEN April 22, 1999
The NBA star was suspected of driving while intoxicated in Houston. He failed a sobriety test but refused a Breathalyzer test. Charges were later dropped.

OZZY OSBOURNE May 15, 1984
Memphis police said the rocker was "staggering drunk" when they arrested him on Beale St. and charged him with public drunkenness.

KEANU REEVES May 5, 1993
Driving erratically in L.A., the actor was pulled over and given a sobriety test. He failed and was charged with DUI.

CARMEN ELECTRA Nov. 5, 1999
Charged with misdemeanor battery after scuffling in a Miami hotel with Dennis Rodman, her ex. A judge ordered the pair to stay away from each other.

AL PACINO Jan. 7, 1961
Long before he perfected the movie mobster, a 20 year-old Pacino was charged in Rhode Island with carrying a concealed weapon.

On the eve of his trial for the murder of Holly Maddux (right), Ira Einhorn vanished—for 16 years.

"I really think the guy felt he could just go off and get away with murder. Einhorn believed the police don't care about a guy who kills his hippie girlfriend. This shows we don't forget about you." **PHILADELPHIA INVESTIGATOR RICHARD DIBENEDETTO**

JUSTICE DELAYED

O n *Law & Order* cops find the corpse, detectives finger a suspect, and Sam Waterston slams the cell door shut in a crisp 60 minutes—commercials included.

In real life the crime-culprit-trial arc often lasts a year or more. Sometimes, in exceptional circumstances, a lot more: 5, 10, even 25 years. Suppressed memories return, science teases new clues from old evidence, investigators painstakingly review stacks of dusty files, and a fresh insight flutters out, a moth with a message.

What drives those cases? Very often the determination of the victims' families, sympathetic cops and public outrage that, somewhere, a killer walks free. In January 2000 Dorthy Moxley received a call from an investigator she had come to know. "Oh, Frank, I'm not going to be disappointed, am I?" she asked. "I think you'll be pleased," he said.

Police had found the man who killed her daughter, Martha, 15, on a quiet fall evening 24 years before,

PEACE, LOVE—AND MURDER

After 16 years on the run, the law finally caught up with fugitive
Ira Einhorn, a groovy '70s guru-turned-killer

N ANTIWAR ACTIVIST AND STAUNCH ENVIRON-
mentalist, Ira Einhorn counted Abbie Hoffman
and Jerry Rubin among his friends. Some saw
him as a visionary; indeed, Einhorn was cred-
ited with being the first to come up with the
idea of Earth Day—a day-long homage to
nature designed to focus people's attention
on the world's pollution problems. An estimated 20 million people participated in that
first event in 1970.

It was just two years later that Helen "Holly" Maddux, a 25-year-old Bryn Mawr College
grad and former cheerleader from Tyler, Texas,
met Einhorn and was smitten. They crossed
paths at Einhorn's favorite Philadelphia hangout, La Terrasse restaurant. Longing to leave
East Texas behind, and much to the dismay
of her parents, she moved in with Einhorn.
But Einhorn's magnetic personality had a dark
side, particularly toward women. Her broth-

Holly "was fascinated with the way Einhorn's mind worked," said a friend of hers.

er John was disgusted at the way Einhorn dominated his sister: "Holly would sit at his feet like a pet or something."

Loyalty seemed to be a one-way street: Einhorn, one friend remembered, often took Holly to parties, then left with other women; he also talked her into having sex with others while he watched. By Labor Day weekend of 1977, Maddux had had enough; she went to New York and became involved with another man. When she returned to Philadelphia to formally break off her relationship with Einhorn, he went ballistic. "She said she had to calm him down," said an assistant district attorney who later handled the case. "Apparently she couldn't."

In mid-September Maddux disappeared. Her family urged police to look into the case, but they found nothing to suggest she had been harmed. Even a private investigator

hired by the family found nothing substantial. It wasn't until March 1979, 18 months later, that neighbors complained of an odor coming from Einhorn's apartment. Armed with a search warrant, police moved in and, guided by the

smell, opened the door to a closet near Einhorn's bedroom. Inside was a steamer trunk, and inside that was Maddux, her body mummified by the heat. She had been killed by several blows to the head with a blunt object.

Einhorn was promptly arrested, but his attorney Arlen Specter, who would later become a prominent U.S. senator, argued that he should be allowed to post bond and remain free until trial. Released on just $40,000 bail, Einhorn returned home. Then, two weeks before his 1981 court date, he vanished. In 1993, after the law was changed to allow trials *in absentia,* Einhorn, still at large, was found guilty of murder.

Meanwhile, police gave chase. Einhorn fled to London, where he stayed with a pal and was joined by a new American girlfriend, Jeanne Morrison. They then rented an apartment in Dublin but slipped away to Wales when they learned police had tracked them down.

Einhorn lived in large part off funds sent him by Barbara Bronfman, whom he had met while organizing Earth Day and who was then married to Charles Bronf-

Einhorn (with Holly in the 1970s) depended on family and friends for his daily needs.

They Killed Her Son; She Nailed the Klan

"I wouldn't want nobody else to go through what I did," said Donald (at her son's grave).

man, heir to the Seagram's fortune. Moving from place to place ahead of the law, Einhorn took on the identity of a Dublin bookseller he had befriended named Eugene Mallon. After Morrison left him, he took up with a new girlfriend, Annika Flodin, the daughter of an affluent Swedish family. The two ultimately settled in the secluded French village of Champagne-Mouton, where they bought a charming two-story mill for about $100,000.

For several years the pair fit almost seamlessly into local society. Flodin ran errands on her bicycle; Einhorn, passing himself off as a mystery writer, joined a bridge club and took an active role in protesting a nearby proposed nuclear power plant. "I never got the feeling they were hiding," said one area resident.

On June 13, 1997, gendarmes surrounded Einhorn's bucolic former mill. Hands on their guns, they rushed through the door, past Flodin and up the stairs, and found Einhorn naked in bed. He protested the intrusion, insisting he was Eugene Mallon and they were making a hideous mistake. Ignoring his pleas, they cuffed him and hauled him off to jail. French officials were taken off guard when the media descended after word of Einhorn's capture. Said one French official: "We had no idea he was some kind of guru."

WHAT HAPPENED: As thrilled as Pennsylvania prosecutors were that Einhorn was behind bars, they were shaken when French authorities refused to extradite him to the U.S. French law forbade trials in absentia, and it was only when Pennsylvania agreed to retry Einhorn that the French released him to the U.S. On Oct. 17, 2002, Einhorn, 62, was found guilty of murder and sentenced to life without parole.

ICHAEL DONALD HAD BEEN OFF VISITING HIS SISTER TWO BLOCKS away, and his mother, Beulah Mae, expected him home by midnight. When he didn't show up, she worried. She sat up all night until the phone rang at 6 a.m. The call was brief and the message terrifying: A young man's body was hanging from a tree in downtown Mobile, Ala., the anonymous voice told her, and she might want to check into it.

It took some time for police to re-create precisely what had happened. Some suspected Michael, 19, had been killed during a drug deal gone bad or by a jealous lover of one of the girls he was dating. In truth, he had left his sister's house and was walking to the corner gas station to buy cigarettes when James "Tiger" Knowles, 17, and Henry Hays, 26, members of the United Klans of America, forced Michael into their car. It was March 1981. A predominantly black jury had recently failed to convict a black man charged with killing a white police officer. Out for revenge, the UKA wanted an eye for an eye.

Imperial Wizard Robert Shelton led the 2,500-member UKA.

Knowles and Hays drove Michael to a remote area outside Mobile, beat him with boards, ran him in circles with a rope around his neck and stomped on him while he pleaded for his life. Then one of the men pulled the rope tight around Michael's neck and the other cut his throat.

The Klan thought they had made their point. They didn't count on Beulah Mae Donald's determination—or on the fact that an insider would tell police what had happened. It took six years, but in 1987 an all-white jury came to a novel conclusion. Rather than simply hold Knowles and Hays to blame, they found the entire organization at fault and ordered the UKA and the six defendants to pay Beulah Mae $7 million in punitive damages. The UKA, which couldn't pay its share, ultimately had to hand over the deed to its two-story national headquarters near Tuscaloosa to Mrs. Donald, 67.

Beulah Mae, in the end, said she never cared about the money, only the truth: "People were telling me, 'There ain't no such thing as the Klan; Michael must have been doing something wrong.' I'm glad it's all come to light."

UPDATE: The civil suit essentially put the UKA out of business. Knowles was also convicted of violating Michael Donald's civil rights and was sentenced to life in prison, and Hays was found guilty of murder and sent to death row. He was executed in 1987.

THE BOY NEXT DOOR

Twenty-seven years after Martha Moxley was beaten to death, Kennedy cousin Michael Skakel was finally held accountable

O THE MOXLEYS, THEIR Belle Haven community seemed the safest place in all of Greenwich, Conn. It had its own security, and the neighborhood was populated by a who's who of affluent families—including their neighbors the Skakels, who were related to the extended Kennedy clan.

So on Oct. 30, 1975, Dorthy Moxley felt no apprehension as her 15-year-old daughter, Martha, bundled up in a blue down jacket and headed out to commit a few pre-Halloween pranks with local kids. Martha, usually responsible, didn't come home when she was supposed to. All night Dorthy stared out the window of the library in the family's sprawling Spanish-style house. It was only the following afternoon, when police began searching the area, that an officer pushed aside low-hanging branches of an evergreen on the Moxley property and discovered Martha's body. Lying face down, Martha had been beaten with a golf club with such force that the club had broken into three parts. Her jeans and underwear were pulled down below her knees, but there was no other evidence of any sexual assault.

In one of the first breaks in the case, police learned that the Skakels across the street owned a set of matching golf clubs and, indeed, the 6-iron was missing. From that moment, investigators zeroed in on the Skakel household. Tommy, 17, was known to have had a crush on Martha. In her diary she had written he kept trying to get to "first and second base" with her. He was also thought to be the last person seen with Martha. Kenneth Littleton, then 23, and a live-in tutor to the Skakel children, also came under suspicion, though no convincing links were found between him and the girl.

Amazingly, the Moxleys and Skakels continued to socialize for a while after the killing, the Moxleys even once visiting their neighbors' ski lodge in Windham, N.Y. But when the Skakels stopped cooperating with police the following year, relations soured, and soon afterward the Moxleys moved away. What frustrated them even more was that the investigation seemed to have run aground.

By and large, even the Skakels managed to get on with their lives—with one exception: Michael, a troubled teenager, struggled with dyslexia and drank heavily. He was even reputed to have beaten squirrels to

"I think of her every day," said Dorthy Moxley of her daughter Martha (in 1974).

death with a golf club. In 1978, when he led police on a drunken high-speed chase, his father sent him to the Elan School in Poland Spring, Maine, a private facility that used a combination of tough love and discipline to rein in rich kids whose lives were spinning out of control.

Evidently, the school failed to work its magic on Michael, who ran away several times and left Elan two years later to spend most of the 1980s on golf courses and ski slopes—as well as in rehab centers. He seemed to get his act together in the 1990s, earning a bachelor's degree, marrying golf pro Margot Sheridan and settling in the affluent Boston suburb of Cohasset, Mass. The Moxley murder had been pushed far into the background.

That changed suddenly in 1991, when William Kennedy Smith, another Kennedy cousin, was tried in West Palm Beach on rape charges. With the limelight back on the clan, new questions were raised about the Moxley murder and the Skakels' involvement. To finally clear his family name, Rushton Skakel, Michael's father, hired a private detective to look into the case. It was a disastrous miscalculation. During questioning, Tommy and Michael dramatically altered their accounts of what had happened that night. Tommy now told the detectives that he and

"You are only as sick as your secrets," Michael Skakel once said, just as a jury was probing his.

The 6-iron used to kill Moxley came from a set of golf clubs in the Skakel household.

Martha had been masturbating each other before parting at around 10 p.m., and Michael said he had climbed a tree outside Martha's bedroom window, where he masturbated.

His interest piqued, Mark Fuhrman, the disgraced former Los Angeles detective famous for his role in the O.J. Simpson case, began personally investigating the case in hopes of writing a book. Fuhrman said that some of Michael's former Elan classmates claimed Michael admitted to them that he had killed Moxley.

When Dorthy Moxley received a call on Jan. 18, 2000, from an inspector with the Connecticut State's Attorney's Office, she said, "Oh,

Frank, I'm not going to be disappointed, am I?" He answered: "I think you'll be pleased."

The next day, Michael Skakel, 39, was charged with Martha's slaying.

WHAT HAPPENED: Skakel suffered a setback when a judge ruled that he would be tried as an adult, even though he was 15 when the murder took place. He seemed to get a break when a key witness, a former Elan student, died of a heroin overdose. But in June 2002, 27 years after the crime, Skakel, who allegedly had told one former friend, "I'm going to get away with murder—I'm a Kennedy," was found guilty and later sentenced to 20 years to life behind bars.

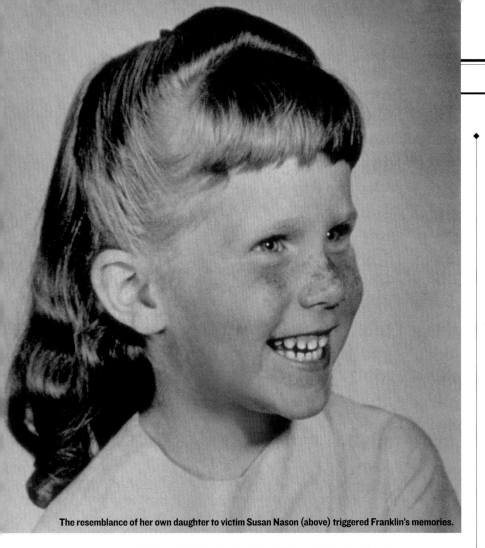

The resemblance of her own daughter to victim Susan Nason (above) triggered Franklin's memories.

Franklin (with her father in the early 1980s) said she endured his abuses for 11 years.

THE SINS OF THE FATHER

SITTING IN HER LIVING ROOM playing with her children, Eileen Franklin had a vision—not of something yet to come, but of a terrifying incident that had taken place 20 years before. It was triggered as she sat in her Canoga Park, Calif., home with her 5-year-old daughter. "Jessica had her head turned up looking at me, and at that moment I saw," said Franklin years later. "The first thing was the silhouette of my father coming with a rock above his head and me holding Susan's gaze." In her mind, as the vision unfolded, Franklin shouted "No!" But what was done so long ago could not be undone.

At first, Franklin, then 28, shared the vision only with her therapist. Then she told her husband, who convinced her to tell police. Suddenly, what had been a horrible memory buried deep in her subconscious became vividly clear.

She was 8 in 1969, when she sat with her father in his van and saw her best friend, Susan Nason, out the window. Eileen invited Susan to join her and her dad in the van, but then something went terribly wrong. Paralyzed by confusion and fear, she watched as her father, George, a fireman from the San Francisco Bay Area, climbed on top of Susan and raped her. Then he hit her, repeatedly, with a rock, until she stopped moving. When he finished, he warned Eileen to keep quiet: After all, he told her, it was her fault for having invited Susan into the van in the first place. Susan's body was not found for another three months, and an investigation turned up no suspects in the killing.

Years later, with those memories released, Eileen began to recall a childhood defined by her father's abuses. He not only beat his wife but sexually abused Eileen (the first time when she was just 3) and at least one of her sisters. On one occasion, her sister told her junior high school teach-ers about the beatings, and police came to the house. They left soon afterward, reassured by George, who also made it very clear to them that he was a fireman.

Eileen had no regrets when police arrested her father, who was found with a collection of child pornography in his apartment, nor for testifying at his trial. "I can live with myself now," she said. "Keeping it in, I don't think I could have."

WHAT HAPPENED: George Franklin Sr. was convicted of murder and sentenced to life. His daughter Eileen is still trying to cope with her recovered memories.

On the witness stand, Franklin showed how her father killed the girl with a rock.

John List shot (from left) daughter Patricia, wife Helen and sons John Jr. and Frederick, then vanished.

Busted by an Artist's Bust

AN ACCOUNTANT BY TRADE, JOHN LIST WAS EQUALly methodical in his personal life. In November 1971 he sat down to write letters to his children's public schools, notifying them that he was taking the family on an extended vacation to North Carolina. He wrote similar notes to the businesses where the kids worked part-time. Then he canceled mail and milk deliveries and drove across the Hudson to JFK International Airport, where he left his car.

Weeks later his neighbors noticed that lights in List's rambling 19-room Victorian home had flickered off one by one. Concerned, they phoned police. James Moran was one of the cops who broke in and made the horrifying discovery: There, neatly laid out side by side, were the Lists: wife Helen, 45, and children Patricia, 16, John Jr., 15, and Frederick, 13. In a separate room lay John's mother, Alma, 85. All had been shot. John List, the patriarch of the family, was nowhere to be found.

Even after he retired in 1986, Chief Moran could not shake the fact that the bloodiest case he had ever investigated had gone unsolved and that, somewhere, John List was living out his days as a free man. Then along came *America's Most Wanted,* the television-age version of post-office "wanted" posters. Sculptor Frank Bender was hired by the show to create a bust of what the 63-year-old fugitive might look like 18 years after the crime.

Bender did a spectacular job. After the program aired, 350 people phoned in tips. One caller furnished the name of Robert P. Clark, which led police to an accountant in Midlothian, Va. Confronted in his office, "Clark" insisted that they were mistaken. But his fingerprints told another story.

List had left a detailed explanation behind when he disappeared. The family's financial troubles, he wrote, had become overwhelming. He had spent nearly all of his mother's savings. He said his wife was drinking heavily, and he feared his daughter was smoking marijuana. Worse than all that, said List, a devout Lutheran, was that he felt his family was slipping away from God. In the five-page letter to his minister, he explained that by "killing them, they would die Christians."

So on Nov. 9, 1971, he loaded two pistols and killed his mother and wife. Then, as each child arrived home from school, he shot them one by one. By sending the letters to the kids' schools and leaving his car at the airport, List hoped to throw off the police. He then set about reinventing his life as Bob Clark. He lived first outside Denver, where he met his second wife, then moved to Virginia for another job. He attended church, gardened, went to movies and lived a peaceful life. Neighbors refused to believe this mild-mannered man could be a murderer. Chief Moran saw it differently: "This bum should never get away with this."

WHAT HAPPENED: List was extradited to New Jersey, where he was tried for the murders of his family, convicted and in May 1990 sentenced to five consecutive life terms.

Eighteen years after the crime, *America's Most Wanted* showed a bust of what List might look like. The uncanny resemblance led to his capture.

Two weeks after police killed six members of the Symbionese Liberation Army in a shootout in Los Angeles, Soliah gave an impassioned speech denouncing cops.

MOM, COOK, TEACHER— AND BOMBER

I T WAS AN UPPER-MIDDLE-CLASS life, and a good one. Sara Jane Olson, a doctor's wife, doted on her three daughters, acted in local theater and was a gracious hostess and gourmet cook. She regularly read to the blind, prepared meals for the homeless and taught English as a second language. Olson was on her way to teach an English class to immigrants on June 16, 1999, when an FBI agent pulled over her gold minivan about a mile from her house. "FBI, Kathleen," he said. "It's over."

For amateur actress Kathleen Soliah, 52, Sara Jane Olson was the role of a lifetime, and she had played it so convincingly that not even her husband suspected she was anything but what she seemed. He certainly never imagined she was a former student

radical and member of the Symbionese Liberation Army, a group famous for having kidnapped Patty Hearst in 1974. Six members of the group were killed that same summer in a shootout with police in Compton, Calif.; in retaliation Olson allegedly planted pipe bombs under two LAPD cruisers. They were discovered and disarmed before they went off, but from that moment on, Soliah was a fugitive in her own country.

In Minnesota she reinvented herself. "She was always doing things for others," said a minister at a church where she narrated the Christmas pageant.

WHAT HAPPENED: Pleading guilty to the attempted bombing and, in a separate case, to her role in a botched bank robbery in which a bystander was killed, she was sentenced to 15 years.

"She's led a quiet, nice life," a neighbor said of Soliah (in '99).

A Perfect Preppy's Life on the Lam

J UST 16 AT THE TIME, SHE WAS worried about breaking her curfew and asked several people at the party for a lift home. Alex Kelly volunteered. The girl had never met him, but he was a handsome high school senior in the affluent suburb of Darien, Conn., so she trusted him. She only began to get nervous when he drove past her parents' house and parked in an isolated cul-de-sac. There, late at night on Feb. 10, 1986, he grabbed her by the throat, forced her into the backseat of the car and threatened to kill her if she didn't have sex with him. "It hurt so bad," she said years later. "It seemed like forever."

She and her parents went to the police, but before authorities could press the case, Kelly fled to Europe. For more than eight years, allegedly with his parents' financial support, Kelly lived the good life, hang-gliding, skiing and partying in Greece, Scandinavia and France. In a letter to his parents, he said he could happily live like that forever. At the same time, he was always looking over his shoulder. "Every day is borrowed time," he wrote his parents, knowing international authorities were hunting him for raping both the girl from the party and another girl who came forward days later.

With police hot on his trail, Kelly finally turned himself in to Swiss authorities and in May 1995 was extradited to the U.S. When the trial for the first alleged rape began in late 1996, the key witness was the victim herself. Though by then a seemingly composed 26-year-old business executive, she broke down several times on the stand. "I asked him, 'Why did he do this to me?'" recalled the

woman, who was never publicly identified because of the nature of the case. "He said he didn't know. He couldn't control himself."

THE VERDICT: In June 1997 Kelly was convicted of rape and sentenced to 16 years. He pleaded no contest to sexual assault in the second case.

Kelly (in custody in the U.S.) was released on bail and worked at his father's plumbing business in the months before the trial. His parents used their home as collateral for the $1 million bail.

A law school drop-out, Bundy (studying legal texts in Colorado in 1979) aided in his own defense.

"What really fascinated him was the hunt, the adventure of searching out his victim. And, to a degree, possessing them physically as one would possess a potted plant, a painting or a Porsche. Owning, as it were, this individual."

TED BUNDY, DESCRIBING THE MOTIVATIONS OF A MURDERER

HEARTS OF DARKNESS

Most killers kill for a reason: lust, anger, revenge, greed. We're familiar with the motives; we've felt them ourselves. Even though we're far too civilized to act, we recognize that, deep down, the perpetrators may be just a little tiny wee bit like us.

But there's one group most of us don't understand: those whose motive for killing is killing itself. They don't hate their victims; often they don't even *know* their victims. When caught, they rarely plead, whine or cry. Frequently they're chillingly matter-of-fact, even boastful. Richard Allen Davis, who murdered Polly Klaas, smirked through much of his trial; serial rapist and murderer Paul Bernardo drily told a jury that, yes, he realized he had a problem with sexuality, adding, "Down the road I'm going to have to seek professional help for it."

Nowadays we call them sociopaths, though some might prefer a shorter, simpler, older word: evil.

"A part of me was hidden all the time," Bundy (right) told his mother the night before he was executed.

ALL-AMERICAN PSYCHO

Beneath Ted Bundy's good looks, intellect and charm lurked a guilt-free killer who murdered at least 20 young women

BY ALMOST ANY MEASURE, TED BUNDY WAS A GREAT KID, with a virtual *Brady Bunch* résumé: Boy Scout, paper route, high school track team; he even ran his own lawn-mowing business. "I admired him tremendously," his sister Linda Bussey said years later. "I always wished I had some of his brains and his knowledge."

And so it went. Young Ted served as Seattle chairman of the New Majority for Rockefeller at the 1968 GOP presidential convention, earned a psychology degree at the University of Washington in 1972 and entered law school at the Uni-

versity of Utah, working nights as a janitor to pay the bills. He even wrote a rape-prevention pamphlet for a Seattle crimewatch group, and once received a letter of gratitude from the Governor of Washington for chasing down a purse snatcher in a shopping mall.

But as well-intentioned, winning and handsome as the six-footer appeared, that was not Ted's whole story. While Bundy lived in Seattle, eight young women were murdered. On July 14, 1974, the day two women vanished, witnesses told police that the victims had been approached, separately, by a man with his arm in a sling. He said his name was Ted and asked for help in hoisting a sailboat onto the roof of his Volkswagen. Neither was seen alive again.

Five months later Carol DaRonch, 18, was abducted in Murray, Utah, by a man claiming to be a police officer. She was suspicious, and even though the man tried to handcuff her and threatened her with a gun, she managed to leap from his car and escape. He chased her with a crowbar but gave up when DaRonch hailed a passing car. Several months after that, a patrol car came upon a parked VW in suburban Granger, Utah, flashed its lights, and the car sped away. Chasing it down, the officer searched the car and found a crowbar, handcuffs and a mask made from pantyhose. The driver, Ted Bundy, was arrested for attempting to evade an officer.

While that case was pending, the arresting officer mentioned Bundy to another officer who was investigating DaRonch's botched kidnapping, as well as the murders of three women in the Salt Lake City area. Weeks before, he had received a call from Liz Kloepfer, Bundy's former girlfriend, who urged Utah police to consider Bundy a suspect in all the killings. She said composite drawings released by police resembled Bundy and that, right around the time two Seattle women had been killed by a man with a cast, she had seen a fake cast in Bundy's apartment. Also, she added, he had once tied her up and nearly choked her to death after she had given him a copy of the book *The Joy of Sex.*

DaRonch had difficulty identifying Bundy; he claimed to have fled from the police because he had been smoking pot and didn't want to jeopardize his law school career. But with

'His only remorse is that he's going to die'

-HUGH AYNESWORTH, A JOURNALIST WHO INTERVIEWED BUNDY BEFORE HIS EXECUTION

spied a reportedly stolen car and pulled it over. At the wheel sat Bundy, who, by then, had earned the dubious distinction of appearing on the FBI's Most Wanted list.

WHAT HAPPENED: Bundy was convicted of murdering the two sorority girls and Kimberly Leach. Though he was suspected in 20, perhaps even 40, other murders, authorities chose to keep

"If I didn't know what I do about him, I'd say he was extremely likable," said sheriff Ken Katsaris (reading Bundy's indictments in Tallahassee in 1979).

little fanfare, he was convicted of kidnapping DaRonch and sentenced to 1 to 15 years.

Bundy was then accused of killing Caryn Campbell, a nurse who disappeared on Jan. 12, 1975, while vacationing near Aspen. Her battered corpse was found in a snowbank five weeks later. Police searching Bundy's apartment during the DaRonch case had found a map of Colorado, the names of two ski lodges underlined in a brochure (the nurse had stayed at one) and credit card receipts proving he was in the Aspen area the day Campbell vanished.

Ted was extradited to Colorado, but the case never went to trial. Bundy

wriggled out of his jail cell through a ventilation duct and fled, ending up in Tallahassee, Fla., where he moved into a rooming house called the Oak.

Shortly after 3 a.m. on Jan. 15, 1978, a man entered Florida State University's Chi Omega sorority house and beat and strangled two women and assaulted two more. Within an hour, a woman living nearby was bludgeoned and raped in her home. Several male Oak residents were suspects in the crimes, but not Bundy. Finally, on Feb. 9, Kimberly Leach, just 12, disappeared from a Lake City, Fla., junior high, about 100 miles east of Tallahassee. Six days later an officer in Pensacola

him in Florida, where he was sentenced to die in the electric chair. Even then the drama didn't stop. Apparently wooed by his uncommon charm, many people, including a Florida TV reporter who investigated the Bundy case, insisted that he was wrongly accused and that any number of other suspects could have committed the crimes.

The courts were not persuaded, but Bundy kept police and judges hopping for years with appeals. On Jan. 24, 1989, his time ran out. As he was being prepared for execution, he unleashed a torrent of new confessions, claiming he had killed in at least four other states. Authorities went ahead with the execution.

CHAMBER OF HORRORS

Murder—and cannibalism—lurked behind the door of apartment 213, home to soft-spoken serial killer Jeffrey Dahmer

TWO OFFICERS WERE ON A ROUTINE PATROL on Milwaukee's rundown west side when a terrified man ran toward them, a pair of handcuffs dangling from one wrist. He told them a man up North 25th Street in apartment 213 had a big knife under his bed and was trying to kill him. Investigating, they knocked at 213. Jeffrey Dahmer, a 31-year-old chocolate-factory worker, opened the door and politely let them in. One officer checked the bedroom and found a knife. He also noticed hundreds of photographs spilling out of a highboy. At first glance they seemed to be photos of nude men.

Then the cops looked more closely: The bodies in the pictures were corpses, mutilated and dismembered. The officers quickly realized that most of the photographs had been taken in that very room. They searched the apartment further. In the refrigerator, on the bottom shelf, was a human head.

The horrors captured in *The Silence of the Lambs* paled in comparison with the real-life story of Dahmer, arguably the most horrifying murderer in United States history. The remains of 11 men turned up in apartment 213. Three more heads were found in a lift-top freezer. Dahmer later confessed that he had saved the frozen body parts to eat later. Bones were stored about the apartment. Police found five full skeletons and five skulls, apparently scraped clean.

Raised in Bath, Ohio, Dahmer came from a broken family and had been sexually abused at age 8 by a male in the neighborhood. He was a peculiar boy who made other kids nervous, especially after they learned he had dismembered and decapitated a dog, mounting the head on a stick next to a wooden cross. His first killing, authorities believe, was in 1978, the year his parents divorced, when he picked up a 19-year-old hitchhiker, took him home and bludgeoned him with a barbell before cutting up the body. In the mid-to-late 1980s, he killed with increasing frequency, luring boys to his grandmother's suburban home or his Milwaukee apartment with the promise of paying them to pose nude. He then drugged them with sedatives, strangled them and dismembered the bodies.

Neighbors remembered bulging bags of trash Dahmer

Dahmer (during his trial) admitted that he had killed at least 15 people. "This is my fault," he told his lawyer. "There is a time to be honest."

was constantly dumping, hearing the whine of a power saw coming from apartment 213, and foul smells wafting under the door. They complained about the odor and he apologized, saying his freezer had broken and all the meat had spoiled.

"He's got this magnetism," Homolka (at their 1991 wedding) said of Bernardo. "I was immediately drawn to him."

Natural Born Killers

I**T WAS A BEAUTIFUL WEDDING. GUESTS DINED ON PHEASANT AND TOASTED THE** happy couple, Paul Bernardo and Karla Homolka, with champagne. At sunset Paul and Karla, so clean-cut that neighbors called them Ken and Barbie, rode off in a horse-drawn carriage. That same afternoon boaters made a grisly discovery: the body—or at least parts of the body—of Leslie Mahaffy, 14. The Ontario teenager had been sexually abused and dismembered with a power saw; her remains had been weighted with concrete and dropped into Lake Gibson, just a few miles from where the wedding was taking place. Mahaffy had last been seen alive two weeks earlier, when her mother, hoping to teach her a lesson about violating her curfew, had locked her out of the house.

Less than a year later, 15-year-old Kristen French vanished on her way home from school. She was found in a ditch, naked, her dark hair shorn. Other local crimes were making news too: From 1987 through 1990, at least 19 women from Toronto to Niagara Falls had been terrorized by a man who had come to be known as the Scarborough Rapist.

Police initially made little progress in the cases—until, seven months after her marriage, Karla Homolka, 23, was admitted to a hospital. She had been beaten and her left eye partially luxated. Homolka blamed the injuries—and more—on her husband. In 1990, she said, she had helped Bernardo drug and rape her 15-year-old sister, Tammy, who then choked to death on her own vomit. Homolka's explanation for her own actions: She hoped his interest in her sister was a passing sexual fantasy. "I still loved him," she said, "and I wanted to make him happy."

The preppy couple (in '89) videotaped their murders.

Then she described to police how Bernardo had kidnapped both Leslie Mahaffy and Kristen French—and how she had stood by with a camera and videotaped him as he raped and tortured the girls.

WHAT HAPPENED: Homolka pleaded guilty to manslaughter and was sentenced to 12 years (she is due for release in July 2005). Bernardo—linked by DNA evidence to 19 sexual assaults—admitted having sex with his victims but denied killing anyone. "Obviously, looking back, I had a problem with sexuality," he said on the stand. He added with a smirk, "Down the road I'm going to have to seek professional help for it."

The prosecution introduced 12 hours of videotape that had been found above a light fixture in Bernardo's house. Viewing the tapes, many in the courtroom wept.

Found guilty of murder, he received a life sentence.

"It was like confronting Satan himself," said Tracy Edwards (above), who barely escaped Dahmer. Police wearing protective suits (below) removed a freezer with various body parts from the apartment.

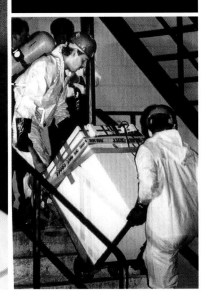

THE VERDICT: Dahmer confessed to 15 murders and pleaded insanity. He was found sane and sentenced to 15 consecutive life terms. Addressing the court, Dahmer insisted, "I hated no one. I knew I was sick or evil or both." In 1994 Dahmer was beaten to death by another prisoner.

AN EVIL ALL ITS OWN

Heartbreaking cases in California, Belgium and England shed light on the unspeakable: crimes against children

RICHARD ALLEN DAVIS: A HUMAN NIGHTMARE

THE JOLTING UNREALITY MUST have made the moment incomprehensible. On an early fall night in the quiet town of Petaluma, Calif., Polly Klaas, 12, was having a sleepover with two friends. At about 10:30, when they went to spread out sleeping bags, she found a stranger with a knife standing in her bedroom. "Which one of you lives here?" demanded the man, who apparently had climbed through a window. Polly said she did; the man tied up her friends and fled with Polly into the night.

In less than an hour, the search was on. Hundreds of locals joined in. Over the next eight weeks, millions of flyers were distributed across the state and beyond; actress Wynona Ryder, who grew up in Petaluma, posted a $200,000 re-

ward. Ninety minutes after the abduction, two Sonoma County deputies, unaware of Polly's disappearance, questioned a man accused of trespassing on a secluded property in Oakmont, 27 miles away, but released him when they found no outstanding warrants.

Two months later, after matching a palm print found in Polly's room, police arrested 39-year-old Richard Allen Davis, a career criminal with a record for assault, armed robbery, burglary and kidnapping. With little emotion Davis confessed that he had strangled the girl and buried her body in an empty field 50 miles away. Then he casually revealed that he had been questioned and released by two cops who had stopped him for trespassing in Oakmont on the night of the kidnapping; it's unlikely that Polly was still alive at the time.

At the trial Davis seemed intent on causing as much pain as possible.

He made a completely unsubstantiated claim that Polly, before he killed her, said she had been sexually abused by her father, Marc Klaas; after his conviction Davis turned, faced Marc and contemptuously thrust both middle fingers into the air. Until his daughter's death and Davis's 1996 trial, Marc said at the time, "I had trouble believing evil exists."

THE VERDICT: Guilty on all counts; he awaits execution in California.

POLICE HEARD CRIES— AND WALKED AWAY

MELISSA RUSSO AND JULIE Lejeune were bright, cheerful 8-year-olds, and their sudden disappearance in June 1995 sent a shudder through Grace-Hollogne, their tiny Belgian hometown. Still, police—hinting at a pattern that would soon inflame the nation—were inexplicably lax about following up leads. As early as September 1995, a woman, Jeannine Lauwens, even called the police to suggest they talk to her son Marc Dutroux, but the call didn't lead to an arrest.

Dutroux, an unemployed electrician, had been convicted in 1989 of kidnapping and raping five young girls. He was sentenced to 13½ years. Astonishingly, he was released in three. He showed no signs of rehabilitation, returning quickly to a life outside the law. With a visible income of $1,300 a month from unemployment benefits, he and his second wife —who, years before, had videotaped Dutroux as he had raped his victims— somehow managed to buy at least six houses. Police suspected he was sell-

"She was really coming into her own," said Marc Klaas, father of Polly (above). Her killer, Davis (left), was defiant throughout the eight-week trial.

"He is not a normal person," Dutroux's own mother said of her son (in custody in 1996).

ing pornography and guns and perhaps trafficking in prostitution. Instead of charging him, however, they simply carted away stolen goods found on his property.

In 1993 police investigating a series of petty crimes took another look at Dutroux, who was renovating his basement. He said he was upgrading the drainage system. In 1995, after police caught Dutroux stealing a car, they searched his house again—and thought they heard children's voices. Dutroux said his three young children were making the noise. The truth: He had actually built a hidden prison chamber in his basement, and the missing 8-year-olds, Julie and Melissa, were locked inside. Cops hauled Dutroux off to prison for car theft; during the three months he was in jail, an accomplice was supposed to provide the girls with food and water. When Dutroux was released, he found one of the girls dead from starvation. The other died soon afterward.

Arrested in August of 1996, after his van was seen near where another girl had disappeared, Dutroux, then 40, broke down during interrogation. He was charged with kidnapping and raping six girls, and murdering two. Shortly after his confession, he led police to his home in Sars-la-Buissiere, where, in the garden, he had buried Julie and Melissa.

THE VERDICT: After Dutroux's arrest, more than 300,000 Belgians took to the streets, outraged at police bungling and demanding justice. Found guilty of the rapes and murders in 2004, Dutroux was sentenced to life behind bars.

THE KILLERS WERE CHILDREN, TOO

DENISE BULGER WAS BUYING sausages in a Liverpool mall when she turned, instinctively, to check on her 2-year-old son, James. He wasn't there. Shoppers and security launched an increasingly frantic search; that night police conducted a house-to-house investigation, and divers searched a nearby canal.

There was no point. Several hours later authorities checking the mall's surveillance cameras came across a grainy image that, in England, would become iconic: A boy, apparently no older than 12, could be seen leading the toddler out of the mall. Two days later, on Feb. 14, 1993, four kids playing by railroad tracks found a mutilated body. James had been beaten with a metal bar and bricks, left on the tracks and cut in half by a passing train. England was stunned when police, acting on a series of tips, arrested two 10-year-olds, Robert Thompson and Jon Venables, for the murder. The boys said they had skipped school to go to the mall and selected James at random. Each fingered the other in the killing.

THE VERDICT: Sentenced to 15 years, Thompson and Venables were released—to British outrage—after serving eight years behind bars.

The convicted 10-year-olds, Jon Venables (top left) and Robert Thompson, were released from a detention center when both were 18 and have since changed their names. A mall security camera captured the haunting image (below) of one of the boys leading 2-year-old James Bulger away.

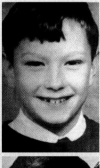

A WOMAN SCORNED (1992)
STARRING: Meredith Baxter as Betty Broderick and Stephen Collins as Dan

After *Family Ties* ended in 1989 and she began edging past the age of cute, Meredith Baxter became something of a TV-movie queen bee, playing ordinary middle-aged women on the verge of . . . doing or enduring something really, really awful. As the San Diego mother of four who killed her ex-husband and his new wife in a jealous rage, she gives a bravura (and Emmy-nominated) performance. A mere seven months later, back by popular demand, Baxter starred in a sequel in which most of the drama was in the title: *Her Final Fury: Betty Broderick, The Last Chapter.*
RATING:

THE PREPPIE MURDER (1989)
STARRING: Lara Flynn Boyle as Jennifer Levin and William Baldwin as Robert Chambers

Back in a more sensitive time—when cheap TV movies about fresh, sensational crimes were still a novel form of entertainment—*Washington Post* critic Tom Shales called this "a faintly sickening exercise in pandering futility." More than 15 years later, it's significant mostly for its leads: Yet another Baldwin brother, William, in his first star performance, and, portraying the woman, Lara Flynn Boyle. The next year she'd be caught up in the murder of Laura Palmer on *Twin Peaks.* **RATING:**

MARTHA INC. (2003)
STARRING: Cybill Shepherd as Martha Stewart

Based on an unauthorized 2002 biography, *Martha Inc.* comes to an end before the home-entertainment tycoon learned that messy legal troubles can't be folded away with the linens. So viewers will feel a certain nostalgia watching the indomitable rise of classic Martha, a bull who could storm a china shop without chipping a cup. Shepherd, a *Martha Stewart Living* subscriber who said she gained some weight for the role and learned to chop, gives a big, vulgar performance, especially when berating underlings. Probably more enjoyable for diva devotees than true-crime lovers. **RATING:**

THE PATTY HEARST STORY (1988)
STARRING: Natasha Richardson as Patty Hearst

In her first major role in a Hollywood film, Richardson plays the heiress turned revolutionary as a blank, aimless American girl who could have as easily been converted to Scientology or Pilates as to the Symbionese Liberation Army. It's a brilliant performance, depressing, oddly funny—maybe satiric. The real, rehabilitated Hearst, by the way, went on to give campy performances in John Waters movies. (Kathleen Turner bludgeons her with a shoe in *Serial Mom.*) **RATING:**

MOVIE ?

A warning to hoodlums: If you don't want a Baldwin to play you on TV, stick to misdemeanors. Put another way: Don't do the crime if you don't want to end up on prime time

MURDER IN NEW HAMPSHIRE (1991)
STARRING: Helen Hunt as Pamela Wojas Smart and Chad Allen as Billy Flynn

The story of a New England schoolteacher who seduced a student and then persuaded him to bump off her inconvenient husband. An adequate dramatization, this was an opportunity for then up-and-coming Hunt to impress audiences with her natural, glinting forcefulness. (The next year, *Mad About You* turned her into a sitcom star.) The same story was reworked into a fictional film, the dark comedy *To Die For,* with Nicole Kidman. **RATING:**

THE DELIBERATE STRANGER (1986)
STARRING: Mark Harmon as Ted Bundy

Harmon, who cemented his heartthrob status playing a doctor on NBC's *St. Elsewhere,* brings a predatory chill to the role of the serial killer (at the time, a convict on death row). Unfortunately—and this is the gruesome irony of a TV movie about serial murder—the drama grows a little less involving as the body count clicks up.
RATING:

BILLIONAIRE BOYS CLUB (1987)
STARRING: Judd Nelson as Joe Hunt

Think of it as a combo platter of two big slices of 1980s American pie: commodities hysteria (Oliver Stone's *Wall Street*) and alienated L.A. youth culture (Bret Easton Ellis's *Less Than Zero*). Nelson, who otherwise probably remains best known for another grouping, *The Breakfast Club*, is the pathologically greedy Hunt, leader of a business-venture-slash-social-club that tries to finance its high-roller style with two murders. Unusually good trial scenes. RATING: 🔫🔫🔫🔫

THE PEOPLE VS. JEAN HARRIS (1982) STARRING: Ellen Burstyn as Jean Harris and Martin Balsam as attorney Joel Aurnou

Not so much ripped from headlines as carefully copied from transcripts, this unusual TV project was shot in four weeks and stuck scrupulously to what had been said during the trial (which is why the credits don't say, for instance, "Telly Savalas as Dr. Tarnower," Tarnower being dead and thus unable to appear in the court proceedings). Harris reportedly didn't like Burstyn's portrayal, thinking it lacked spirit. The scandal will be revisited in an upcoming movie, *Mrs. Harris,* starring Annette Bening and (as Tarnower) Ben Kingsley. RATING: 🔫🔫🔫

GETTING AWAY WITH MURDER (2000)
STARRING: Julia Granstrom as JonBenét Ramsey

Timing is everything—in life, programming and even murder, while taste counts for not much. FOX raced this tacky one-hour docudrama onto the air the week before CBS broadcast its own Ramsey movie, the four-hour *Perfect Murder, Perfect Town* (which didn't get great reviews either). RATING: 🔫

THE POSITIVELY TRUE ADVENTURES OF THE ALLEGED TEXAS CHEERLEADER-MURDERING MOM (1993)
STARRING: Holly Hunter as Wanda Holloway

The fact that the title's terms *positively true* and *alleged* cancel each other out tells you something about the kidding tone of this HBO movie. As the mom who may have taken cheerleading far too seriously, Hunter is fiercer than a ferret. RATING: 🔫🔫🔫

HONOR THY FATHER AND MOTHER (1994)
STARRING: David Beron, Billy Warlock, Jill Clayburgh and James Farentino as the Menendez family

The highlight of this **FOX** film (**CBS** did one too) is the scene in which Kitty Menendez rips the toupee off son Lyle's bald head. Killing your parents is primal drama, sure, but denuding your son's head deserves to be enshrined in Freudian myth. Susan Blakely, one of the TV movie's *grandes dames*, plays attorney Leslie Abramson with perfect frizz. Just so-so, though, in making any sense of the case. **RATING:** 🔫

THE PERFECT HUSBAND (2004)
STARRING: Dean Cain as Scott Peterson, Tracy Middendorf as Amber Frey

Lois & Clark's Superman Cain bears a strong likeness to supercreep Scott Peterson, but the actor who would have been perfect—with a handsomeness so conventional it suggests something unconventional might be simmering deep within—would have been Ben Affleck. If only Affleck's Hollywood career had sunk to USA Network movies! This quickie was shot before the Peterson murder trial began, so there's a lot of pussy-footing around the evidence. **RATING:** 🔫🔫

From left to right:

The Amy Fisher Story (1993) **Drew Barrymore & Anthony John Denison**

Casualties of Love: The Long Island Lolita Story (1993) **Alyssa Milano & Jack Scalia**

Amy Fisher: My Story (1992) **Noelle Parker and Ed Marinaro**

Know Your Buttafuocos

In the space of just a few months—well, in the case of **CBS** and **ABC**, the same night—the networks all dramatized the Amy Fisher scandal, only from different viewpoints—the *Rashomon* of the Long Island Expressway. **NBC**'s *Amy Fisher: My Story,* based in part on Fisher's memoir, makes Joey Buttafuoco out to be a dangerous jerk, all the way from forcing Amy to work as a call girl to giving a thumbs-up to talk about Amy shooting his wife, poor Mary Jo. (Amy's best line: "He loves me, we have great sex, and he fixes my car.") **CBS**'s *Casualties of Love,* for which the Buttafuocos were paid a reported $300,000, makes nice to Joey and trashes Amy as a cold-blooded nutcase. **ABC**'s *Amy Fisher Story* (**RATING:** 🔫🔫🔫) is probably the one that counts, simply because it happens to star 18-year-old Drew Barrymore. And includes this line: "If it wasn't for his wife, we'd definitely be going to the prom together."

"To the killers of JonBenét Ramsey, each day brings us closer to the day when you will reap what you have sown."

COLORADO GOV. BILL OWENS, OCT. 27, 1999. HER KILLER REMAINS AT LARGE.

MYSTERIES & SUDDEN TWISTS

Crime & punishment: They go together like ham & eggs. Or vodka & blinis. Ask Dostoyevsky.

But that's fiction. In real life—even in front-page cases, and despite money, experts, DNA labs, tantalizing evidence and squadrons of cocksure, well-coiffed TV talking heads—some crimes remain maddeningly unresolved. In the case of JonBenét Ramsey, murdered in 1996, a grand jury looked at more than 122 suspects—and no charges were filed. Town bully Ken Rex McElroy terrified tiny Skidmore, Mo.—until someone shot him dead, on Main Street, in front of 60 witnesses. Yet when police asked questions, no one remembered seeing a thing.

In other celebrated cases—Claus von Bülow's, for example—the jury concluded that, in fact, no crime had been committed. With the rap of a judge's gavel, a whodunnit became a wasanythingreallydun?

LITTLE GIRL LOST

Plagued by a cloud of suspicions and police missteps, the investigation into the murder of JonBenét Ramsey comes up empty

"She was always so bubbly, always smiling," a neighbor said of JonBenét (in 1995).

The Ramsey's elegant 6,800-sq.-ft. home in Boulder, Colo., had a separate catering kitchen, a retractable movie screen in the master bedroom and pricey antiques.

HE DAY AFTER CHRISTMAS 1996, PATSY RAMSEY, 40, ROSE early and was on her way down to the kitchen of her family's Boulder, Colo., home when she found a three-page, hand-printed note on the steps. She read the words in disbelief. It was a ransom note claiming that her 6-year-old daughter JonBenét, a veteran of countless "Little Miss" beauty pageants, had been kidnapped and would be returned safely only if the Ramseys coughed up $118,000. Dashing up the stairs, she threw open the door to JonBenét's bedroom, only to find an empty bed.

Police arrived shortly after Patsy phoned 911, and they and the family waited patiently for the call promised in the note. It never came. Around 2 p.m., just after police had gone to get a routine search warrant for the Ram-

sey house, Patsy's husband, John, 53, a computer executive, ventured into the basement. When he flicked on the light, there she was. Dressed in long, white underwear and a white shirt with a sequined silver star, JonBenét lay on the floor with tape over her mouth and a cord wrapped tightly around her neck.

The investigation that followed alternately saddened and enraged the nation. Images of JonBenét were ubiquitous—many taken at pageants, her tiny face framed by carefully coiffed hair and her features highlighted by disturbingly adult applications of rouge, lip gloss and mascara.

Forensic reports concluded that JonBenét had been bludgeoned before she was strangled. She may also have been sexually molested. As devastated as Patsy and John appeared, investigators couldn't help but eye them warily. There was no hard evidence that anyone had broken into the house, and no one had visited. The ransom note also seemed to have been written on paper taken from a legal pad in the

> Mr. Ramsey,
>
> Listen carefully! We are a group of individuals that represent a small foreign faction. We do respect your bussiness but not the country that it serves. At this time we have your daughter in our posession. She is safe and unharmed and if you want her to see 1997, you must follow our instructions to the letter.
>
> You will withdraw $118,000.00 from your account. $100,000 will be in $100 bills and the remaining $18,000 in $20 bills. Make sure that you bring an adequate size attache to the bank. When you get home you will put the money in a brown paper bag. I will call you between 8 and 10 am tomorrow to instruct you on delivery. The delivery will be exhausting so I advise you to be rested. If we monitor you getting the money early, we might call you early to arrange an earlier delivery of the
>
> money and hence a earlier delivery pick-up of your daughter. Any deviation of my instructions will result in the immediate execution of your daughter. You will also be denied her remains for proper burial. The two gentlemen watching over your daughter do particularly like you so I advise you not to provoke them. Speaking to anyone about your situation, such as Police, F.B.I., etc., will result in your daughter being beheaded. If we catch you talking to a stray dog, she dies. If you alert bank authorities, she dies. If the money is in any way marked or tampered with, she dies. You will be scanned for electronic devices and if any are found, she dies. You can try to deceive us but be warned that we are familiar with Law enforcement countermeasures and tactics. You stand a 99% chance of killing your daughter if you try to out smart us. Follow our instructions
>
> and you stand a 100% chance of getting her back. You and your family are under constant scrutiny as well as the authorities. Don't try to grow a brain John. You are not the only fat cat around so don't think that killing will be difficult. Don't underestimate us John. Use that good southern common sense of yours. It is up to you now John!
>
> Victory!
>
> S.B.T.C

Although handwriting experts hired by investigators determined that John Ramsey was not the author of this ransom note left at the crime scene, Patsy was never ruled out.

house, and a stick used to twist the cord around her neck had been broken off one of Patsy's paintbrushes.

Suspicions ran higher four days after the murder, when the parents hired individual criminal attorneys. They soon added a private investigator and public relations expert. They also refused to give police a formal taped interview—a right they could exercise because they had not been charged. Some family acquaintances even wondered privately if JonBenét's brother Burke, then 9, had been jealous of his sister—perhaps because of all the attention his parents had lavished on her.

Over the next several months and beyond, the Ramseys, despite repeated professions of innocence, became objects of intense scrutiny and speculation. They moved to Atlanta, where the couple had met and near where JonBenét was buried with her teddy bear, and later to Michigan, where John ran

unsuccessfully for the state legislature. Police took abuse for initially mishandling the case—for example, by allowing John Ramsey to contaminate the crime scene by carrying JonBenét's body upstairs.

WHAT HAPPENED: On Oct. 13, 1999, a Boulder County grand jury was disbanded after sitting for 13 months and considering, and rejecting, more than 122 suspects. No charges have ever been filed.

In 1997 the Ramseys made a tearful plea and offered a $100,000 reward for any information leading to an arrest and conviction in the murder of their daughter.

Crane (with Werner Klemperer, right, and John Banner in *Hogan's Heroes*) liked to tell people, "A day without sex is a day wasted."

SEX, MURDER AND VIDEOTAPE

THE CURTAIN CAME DOWN, THE audience applauded, and the actor may have ruefully wondered why. Did they like his performance in the show—a frothy comedy called *Beginner's Luck* at the Windmill Dinner Theater in Scottsdale, Ariz.—or did they recall him from his years as the rakish Colonel Hogan on the classic lighter-side-of-life-in-a-Nazi-POW-camp sitcom *Hogan's Heroes*? Either way, actor Bob

Crane, 49, was no doubt painfully aware of how far his career had fallen.

That night—June 28, 1978—after the show, he met up with a friend, John Henry Carpenter. The two went to a local nightspot, then took two women to dinner. At about 2:30 a.m., the party broke up, and Crane retired, alone, to his sublet apartment.

The next afternoon Victoria Berry, Crane's *Beginner's Luck* costar, arrived to

get his help with an audition tape she was making. She knocked but got no answer. The door was unlocked, so she walked in and went looking for Crane. She found him in bed, dead, his face bloodied and an electric cord tied around his neck.

The investigation would reveal, among other things, that there was a dark, or at least kinky, side to the beloved comedy actor. A cache of snapshots and videotapes showed Crane having sex with scores of women—one video showed both Crane and Carpenter engaging in

"I'm so relieved," said Carpenter, who was acquitted but lost his job while awaiting trial.

sex with a young woman. The video-equipment salesman had supplied Crane with all the latest audio-visual devices and had played Crane's sidekick on their quests to conquer and film more and more women.

Although the murder had been violent, the killer left virtually no clues. Police focused on Carpenter after they learned that he had checked out of his hotel and flown to L.A. on the morning Crane's body was found. A waitress told police she had heard the two men in a heated argument two nights before the murder. And police found what they thought might be a speck of Crane's tissue in a car Carpenter had rented.

It took 16 years, but prosecutors finally brought Carpenter to court in 1994. They claimed he had beaten Crane to death with a tripod because the actor had ended their friendship, which meant Carpenter no longer had easy access to women. But after an eight-week trial, Carpenter was acquitted.

FINAL WORD: "There wasn't any proof," said one juror. "You can't prove someone guilty on speculation."

A Writer Seeks Peace, Finds Violence

EIGHBOR TIM ARNOLD, DROPPING BY TO RETURN A FLASH-light, looked through the open door and froze. What he saw was heartbreaking: Christa Worthington, 46, a fashion writer who had moved to quiet Truro, Mass., to get away from Manhattan's big-city pace, lay dead on the floor of her cottage; her daughter Ava, 2, clung to her mother's bloodied, pajama-clad body. An investigation revealed that Worthington's back door had been kicked open, that she had been stabbed in the chest, and that she might have been dead as long as 36 hours. Police initially questioned Arnold, a children's book author who briefly lived with Worthington, and Tony Jackett, then 51, a married local fisherman who proved to be Ava's father. They were never charged, and the murder—which occurred in January 2002—remained a mystery.

UPDATE: In April 2005 police charged Christopher McCowen, 33, an ex-con who had collected Worthington's garbage, with her murder. Authorities said DNA from McCowen—collected in 2004 but not tested until 2005—matched semen found on the victim's body.

Police seemed stymied after DNA tests failed to link two men who had been involved with Worthington to the crime.

"You don't forget this 6'4" witty man," a friend said of Von Bülow (in 1985). "He has presence."

PROUDLY NOTORIOUS

A jury found Claus von Bülow guilty of murder. A second set him free. Win or lose, the society playboy reveled in celebrity

THEY SEEMED TO LEAD a life straight from the pages of Henry James. On a typical languid day, Sunny and Claus von Bülow strolled the grounds of their Newport, R.I., estate and, after a quiet lunch, napped with their four Labradors draped over the bed, then entertained friends at lavish dinners presented by their liveried staff. Over the years, though, gradually and inexplicably, Sunny began to withdraw from high society. "I got the feeling no one saw much of Sunny except the servants," recalled one friend.

Gossip about the von Bülows and what seemed to be their disintegrating marriage roared to the fore on Dec. 27, 1979, when Sunny, found unconscious in the house, was whisked off to Newport Hospital, where she was revived. Almost exactly a year later, on Dec. 21, Sunny failed to appear for breakfast. "Where's Mother?" asked Alex, one of Sunny's children from a previous marriage. Claus claimed to have risen early to let out the dogs and hadn't returned to his bedroom. When they checked, they found Sunny lying, in her nightgown, face down on the bathroom floor.

As Sunny, 49, the only child of a Pittsburgh socialite and her wealthy husband, lay in a coma from which she was never expected to recover, investigators zeroed in on von Bülow, a dashing gadabout and former aide to John Paul Getty. With rumors of alcoholism, infidelity, disputed wills and spiteful stepchil-

dren swirling around the monied parlors of Newport, police ultimately rejected von Bülow's explanation that his deeply neurotic wife had caused her own problems. Her first episode, he said, was set off by her own indulgent combination of boozy egg nog and barbiturates; her second, a case of hypoglycemic shock, was caused by an ice-cream sundae. But police insisted that von Bülow was infatuated with both a vivacious young soap-opera actress and his wife's millions and had attempted to kill Sunny by injecting her with insulin.

During the course of his seven-week trial in 1982, von Bülow attracted fans. Women reached out to touch him as he entered the courthouse, and a vendor sold Claus T-shirts. But whatever charisma he

Von Bülow and Andrea Reynolds, his companion at the time, celebrated his 1985 acquittal.

exercised, the jury was not swayed. After a contentious deliberation, they returned a verdict of guilty.

THE SEQUEL: The original verdict was thrown out because of inconsistencies in the medical and scientific evidence. During the 1985 retrial, the defense refuted claims that Sunny had been felled by insulin injections, and von Bülow was acquitted. Outraged, Sunny's family filed a civil suit against von Bülow, which he settled in 1988, agreeing to divorce his wife and abandon any claim to her estate.

Claus von Bülow can still be seen wearing his signature black-leather motorcycle jacket in London, where he writes theater criticism, hosts parties at his club, and lives the good life. By contrast, Sunny remains in a coma, her body hunched in the fetal position in a New York nursing home. A hairdresser and beautician visit her frequently, and once a week a pianist plays for her, though, in truth, no one believes she can hear the music.

Early in their marriage, Claus and Sunny (in 1968) were fixtures of high-society parties.

Levy hoped to come back to D.C., perhaps to work at one of the agencies.

The Intern, The Politician— And Unanswered Questions

ing her cell-phone records, police found little of interest—except a series of calls Levy had placed to Gary Condit, the seven-term Congressman from her district. When police heard from Chandra's friends that she had a secret and powerful lover, they grew more suspicious.

For weeks Condit played cat and mouse with the media, acknowledging that he knew Levy but refusing to concede they had ever had an intimate relationship. He said he considered her a friend and that they would sometimes discuss articles she had read on the Internet. The last time they met, he said, was on April 24 at his condo, where they

> '**I've probably done more in terms of cooperating with the authorities than anyone in Washington, D.C.**'

L IKE THOUSANDS OF CAREER-minded twentysomethings, Chandra Levy came to Washington, D.C., in the fall of 2000 to get a taste of public service and to make connections. So she was disappointed when her internship at the Federal Bureau of Prisons was expiring in the spring of 2001 and she hadn't landed a permanent job. Planning to return home to Modesto, Calif., she canceled a health-club membership, e-mailed her flight plans to her parents and began packing.

She was last seen on April 30, and it wasn't until May 7 that police, called by Levy's concerned parents, entered her apartment and found her bags, cell phone and wallet—but no sign of Chandra. Searching everywhere and everything, includ-

"I didn't do anything," Wells pleaded, with a bomb locked to his neck.

talked about her future job prospects and promised one another to stay in touch.

Rightly or wrongly, all the attention took its toll on Condit, who had routinely won reelection with ease but who was soundly turned out by voters in his next primary.

WHAT HAPPENED: One year later, on May 22, 2002, police found Chandra's skeletal remains in Rock Creek Park. An autopsy determined that Levy had been murdered, but no cause of death could be established. No one has ever been indicted in the case, and police were unable to link Gary Condit to her disappearance.

Police searched Condit's home but never formally named him as a suspect.

A HUMAN TIME BOMB

A LWAYS RELIABLE, BRIAN WELLS ARRIVED AT 2 P.M. ON AUG 28, 2003, for his delivery job at Mama Mia's pizza. Soon he was out the door, en route with an order for two small pepperoni pies. Forty minutes later Wells, 46, approached a teller at a PNC Bank branch near Erie, Pa., and, saying he had a bomb, demanded $250,000. The instant he stepped out of the bank, police, already alerted, surrounded him and forced him to sit in the road. Wells called out that he was innocent and that he had been forced by someone else to rob the bank. He did have a bomb, though—and it was locked to his neck by a metal collar. It was set to detonate in 20 minutes.

"Why is it nobody's trying to get this off me?" he cried out. "I don't have a lot of time."

The bomb squad arrived too late. Just as Wells had warned, the bomb blew up, killing him instantly.

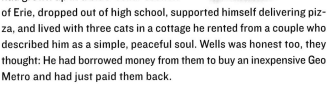

The unusual collar holding the bomb was made of three metal bands.

Police were mystified. Checking Wells's background, they learned he had grown up in a blue-collar section of Erie, dropped out of high school, supported himself delivering pizza, and lived with three cats in a cottage he rented from a couple who described him as a simple, peaceful soul. Wells was honest too, they thought: He had borrowed money from them to buy an inexpensive Geo Metro and had just paid them back.

Chasing down what few leads they had, police learned that the address Wells had been given for delivering the two pizzas was bogus. They also heard reports that two men were seen acting suspiciously near the bank moments before the robbery. Investigators also found two notes, one that was shown to the teller and the other detailing instructions for robbing a bank. The strange metal collar that secured the bomb to Wells's neck was like nothing police had ever seen. In the end, remarked a woman who witnessed Wells's death, "Nobody knew if he was a good guy or a bad guy."

WHAT HAPPENED: No arrests have ever been made.

Town bully Ken Rex McElroy (right) was shot in broad daylight on the main street of Skidmore, Mo. (above), in front of dozens of witnesses—but none remembered seeing anything.

The Town That Saw Nothing

FOR THE PEOPLE OF SKIDMORE, Mo., Ken Rex McElroy was a walking nightmare. A hulk with a hair-trigger temper and a deep love of firearms, he had been in trouble with the law since his teen years and had almost always beaten the rap. Then one day a grocery store clerk accused McElroy's daughter of stealing a piece of candy. McElroy became enraged, retrieved a shotgun and blasted the clerk in the neck. The man survived, but a jury found McElroy guilty of assault, and the town, collectively, breathed a huge sigh of relief.

Then a judge released McElroy on bail, pending his appeal.

On the morning of July 10, 1981, McElroy was scheduled to appear in court on charges that he had violated his bond agreement— by walking into the local D&G tavern carrying a .30-cal. Army carbine with a bayonet. At the same moment, about 60 Skidmore residents were meeting with the mayor and county sheriff to figure out what could be done about taming McElroy. They were debating options when they got word that McElroy and his wife, Trena, had just pulled in and were having a drink at the D&G.

The meeting adjourned to the street.

McElroy's 13-year-old son Juarez (in 1981) had nightmares after his father was shot.

When Ken Rex and Trena emerged from the bar and climbed into their pickup, the crowd followed slowly. Then Trena glanced back and shouted a warning, "They've got a gun!" An instant later, shots rang out. McElroy's head lurched forward, hit by a bullet fired from a high-powered rifle. He died instantly.

Trena identified the shooter as Del Clement, co-owner of the D&G. But even though there were dozens of eyewitnesses, no one else came forward with helpful testimony. The town kept its silence, and a coroner's jury declined to issue an arrest warrant.

Law enforcement officials across the nation were infuriated by the vigilante justice, as was McElroy's wife, though she conceded that in the moment before her husband was shot, "I think he kind of knew what was going to happen. He didn't show any fear. He never said a word." Echoing the sentiments of most residents, however, one D&G regular said, "The only surprise to me is that Ken Rex lived as long as he did."

WHAT HAPPENED: No one has ever been charged.

AU PAIR FREED IN A REVERSAL OF FORTUNE

"HELP! THERE'S A BABY!" the young voice cried, imploring the emergency operator to send help. "He's barely breathing!"

A medical team raced to the Newton, Mass., home of Sunil Eappen, 31, an anesthesiologist, and his wife, Deborah, 32, an ophthalmologist. There technicians found 8-month-old Matthew and his distraught nanny Louise Woodward. Just 18, from the English hamlet of Elton, Woodward said she had entered Matthew's bedroom to rouse him from his nap and found him barely conscious. Terrified, she tried to revive him with mouth-to-mouth resuscitation. When that didn't work, she said, she shook him a little bit.

Matthew was rushed to Boston's Children's Hospital, where doctors found internal bleeding and a 2½-inch fracture at the back of his skull. Five days later, with Matthew in a coma, the Eappens requested he be taken off life support. By that time, Woodward was in custody, and she was soon charged with murder. Essentially, police said, she had shaken Matthew to death.

Two portraits emerged of the inexperienced nanny. Supporters praised her gentle nature, noting that she was lighthearted (nicknamed Loopy Loo for her humor) and had become a vegetarian in her early teens because she cared so deeply for living creatures. But during the trial, the Eappens and others denounced her as irresponsible, citing, for instance, the fact that she had violated her curfew several times, spending too much of her time in Boston bars.

The courtroom drama reached an even higher pitch when EF Au Pair, the referral company where the Eappens found Woodward, hired Barry Scheck of O.J. "dream team" fame to defend her. Scheck argued that Matthew's death could have been the result of an earlier, unexplained skull fracture that began to rebleed after a minor shaking. Scheck's magic failed to dazzle this time, and on Oct. 30, 1997, a jury found Woodward guilty of murder. Advocates on both side of the aisle wailed in outrage. Woodward herself cried out, "I didn't do anything... I'm only 19!"

WHAT HAPPENED: Although the second-degree murder conviction carried a sentence of at least 15 years, Judge Hiller Zobel exercised his prerogative and reduced the murder charge to manslaughter, explaining that Woodward had hurt Matthew not out of malice but out of "confusion" and "immaturity." He sentenced Woodward to time served (279 days). As soon as prosecution appeals were exhausted, Woodward boarded a plane bound for home.

"I really, truly hope that [Louise] can face up to what she has done," said Sunil Eappen (above, with his wife, Deborah), referring to the death of their son Matthew (left). Woodward (below) reacts to the verdict.

"How can they do that to me?" Louise Woodward (in 2000) said after the verdict.

Don Lewis Disappeared
(Does That Cat Look Fat?)

Carole Lewis (playing with her leopard Armani) said her husband had such a passion for big cats that he bought every "abused, dying, maimed cat he could find."

Though wealthy, Don gave Carole a $14 wedding ring when they married in 1991.

DON LEWIS'S DAUGHTER thought the police had made a crucial error: "We were upset that the cops didn't test the DNA on the meat grinder."

Perhaps an explanation is in order. On Aug. 18, 1997, Don Lewis, a self-made millionaire, went missing. Police soon found his van at an airport near his Tampa home. After that, nothing.

Lewis, 60, and his second wife, Carole, then 36, had transformed 40 acres of Tampa real estate into a refuge for 200 leopards, cougars and other big cats. In her remark about the meat grinder, Donna Pettis, one of Lewis's daughters from his first marriage, was suggesting, not subtly, that perhaps Carole very much knew what had happened to her husband, and the cats did too.

Nonsense, said Carole: "My tigers eat meat; they don't eat people." No trace of Don Lewis was ever found—leaving Carole and his children to battle over control of his $5 million estate.

HAVE YOU SEEN THIS MAN?

MISSING

HEIGHT: About 20 inches **COMPLEXION:** Green **EYES:** Wide, and yellow.

DISPOSITION: Very, very nervous. With, apparently, some justification.

LAST SEEN: Hanging on a wall in Oslo, Norway's Munch Museum, on Aug. 22, 2004. Two armed thieves allegedly grabbed him and ran off.

VALUE: $70 million.

UPDATE: In April, 2005, Norwegian police charged two suspects in connection with the theft of The Scream, and said there was a good chance the painting would be recovered—although that "could take some time."

COVER (clockwise from top left) Modesto Bee/Polaris; Reuters/Landov; Randall Simons/Polaris; John T. Barr

BACK COVER (clockwise from top left) Nashville Police/AP; Steve Granitz/Wireimage; Splash News; California Highway Patrol/Getty; Austin Police/AP; Sarasota Police/AP; Aiken County Sheriff/AFP; Splash News (2)

CONTENTS 8-9 Getty/Colin Anderson

IN COLD BLOOD 10-11 Courtesy Rocha Family 12-13 (from left) Getty (2); Polaris 14-15 (from left) Polaris; Reuters/Landov; Chris Hardy/San Francisco Chronicle/Corbis Saba 16-17 (clockwise from left) G.W. Miller III/Philadelphia Daily News; Robert Ruiz/Sipa; Corbis Sygma; AP 18-19 (from left) Helmut Newton/CPI; Ipol; Steve Liss; AP 20-21 (from left) Zuma; Desert Morning News/Getty 22-23 (clockwise from left) Zuma; AP (4) 24 (clockwise) David Harple/New Times (3) 25 (from left) AP; Dick Moran/Union Leader; AP

THE UNUSUAL SUSPECTS 26-27 Doug Menuez 30-31 (from left) Lou Toman/Sun Sentinel; Geoff Willkinson; Dale Wittner; Court TV 32-33 (from left) Cynthia Johnson/Time Life/Getty; Terry Arthur/Camera 5 (5); Norm Hamilton 34-35 (from left) Richard Hammond/Pensacola News Journal; Dale Wittner; CBS Photo Archive 36-37 (from left) Zigy Kaluzny; Boston Herald 38-39 (from left) Alan Jacobson/Morning Call; Jim Mone/AP; Keri Pickett 40-41 (clockwise from left) Richard Howard/Camera 5 (2); Wm. Franklin McMahon; Najlah Feanny/Corbis Saba (2)

CRIMES OF PASSION 42-43 Allan Tannenbaum/Polaris 44-45 (clockwise from left) Corbis Sygma; John Vink/Contact Press; NY Daily News; Newsday 46-47 (clockwise from left) James M. Parcell; Mary Ellen Mark; Jim Powers/Inquirer and Mirror; Victoria Arocho/AP; John Chiasson; Ken Lambert 48-49 (from left) Ron Galella; Arthur Schatz/Getty; AP 50-51 (from left) Wilbur Fuches/Gannet Westchester Papers; Mark Lennihan/AP; AP; Paul Natkin; Joe Juarez/Oakland Press 52-53 Jim McHugh (2) 54 (from left) Portraits by Gerald (2); AP 55 (from top) Globe/NBC; Cheung Ching Ming; Steven Long 56-57 (clockwise from left) Sarah Greenhalgh/AP; Marianne Barcellona/Getty; Dick

Yarwood/Newsday; Melissa Jones/Retna; Mary McLoughlin/NY Post/Rex USA; Sipa

STRANGER THAN PULP FICTION 58-59 Sake Rijpkima 60-61 (from bottom left) Yannis Kontos/Corbis Sygma (2); Linda Best/Bozeman Daily Chronicle 62-63 (clockwise from left) John Holmberg/Seattle Post-Intelligencer; Andrew Kaufman/Contact Press; Rich Frishman/Getty 64-65 (clockwise from left) Boyd Anderson Photography; Michael Pearlman/Christopher Michael Photography; Jim Estrin/New York Times; Denis Poroy/AP; Dave Gatley/Los Angeles Times 66-67 (clockwise from left) Sam Kittner; Chris Tyreel/Star Democrat; Courtesy Superior Court of Arizona; Courtesy WBAL-TV

FOLLOW THE MONEY 68-69 Wayne Wilcox Studio 70 (from top) John T. Barr (2) 71 Liverpool Daily Post & Echo 72-73 (clockwise from left) AP; Eric Strachan/Naples Daily News; Lancaster New Era; Fayetteville Observer (3); Broward County Sheriff's Dept.; Lancaster New Era 74-75 (from left) AP (2); New York Daily News (2) 76 (from top) Robert Kalfus; Courtesy Generosa Ammon Estate; New York Daily News 77 (from top) Axel Koester/Corbis Sygma; Steve Marcus/Las Vegas Sun (3)

HOLLYWOOD & CRIME 78-79 (clockwise from left) Ethan Miller/Corbis; Steve Granitz/Wireimage; Stephen Chernin/Getty; Fernando Allende/Celebrity Photo; Adam Scull/Photolink; Al Rendon/Ida Mae Astute/ABC/Reuters; C. Strong 80-81 Gregg Deguire/Wireimage 82-83 (clockwise from left) Joseph Villarin/AP; Neal Preston; Reuters/Landov; AP 84-85 (clockwise from left) Bob Schafer; David McNew/Getty; Dean Michaels/Rex USA; Almasio & Cavicchioni/Grazia Neri; AP 86-87 (from left) Visages; AP 88 J.P.Owen/Blackstar 89 Nick Ut/AP; Juan Carlo/Ventura County Star/AP 90-91 (clockwise from left) Harry Benson; David McGough/DMI; Anthony Savignano/Galella; Lannis Waters/Corbis Sygma/AP; Lynne Sladky/AP 92-93 Carlo Allegri/Getty 94-95 (clockwise from right) Eric Neitzel/Wireimage; Mylan Ryba/Globe; Granada/ABC 96-97 (clockwise from left) Catherine McGann/Corbis Outline; Andrea Renault/Globe; NY News Service; Deb Carvalho/Filmmagic; Lisa Rose/Globe 98-99 (clockwise from left) Bob Sacha; Jim Selby/Globe; Getty; Albert L. Ortega/Wireimage;

Lori Shepler/LA Times/AP; Neal Preston/Corbis Outline; Courtesy Samantha Gailey Geimer 100-101 (clockwise from left) John Dyer; Paul Harvath/Corbis Sygma; Intersport TV; Brent Wojahn/Corbis Sygma (2); Tom Fox/Corpus Christi Caller/Getty

FAMOUS MUGS 102-103 (clockwise from left) Splash News; Teaneck Police; Royal Oak Police; AP; Big Pictures; Pacific Coast News; Nick Ut/AP; Ho/AP; LA Bureau; Steve Granitz/Wireimage; California Highway Patrol/Getty; AP; Rex USA; LA Bureau; Austin Police/AP 104-105 (clockwise from left) Splash News; Reuters/Landov; Zuma; AP (5); Sipa; Splash News; Wilmington Police Dept.; Splash News; AFP; AP (2); Splash News; AP

JUSTICE DELAYED 106-107 William Thomas Cain/Getty 108-109 Pascal Saura/Corbis 110 Zuma (2) 111 (from top) Peter Serling; Burk Uzzle 112-113 (from left) AP; Getty; Andrade Patrick/Gamma 114 (from top left) Courtesy Helen Brann Agency (2); John Green 115 (from top) AP; Paul Fedders; AP 116 (from top left) AP (2); Jennifer Bishop 117 (from top) Andrea Renault/Globe; Andy Levin

HEARTS OF DARKNESS 118-119 ©Seattle Times 120-121 George Kochaniec Jr. (4) 122-123 (from left) Allen Fredrickson/Reuters/Corbis; AP; Photo News; Jack Orton/Milwaukee Journal/Sipa 124-125 (clockwise from left) Canada Wide; PA; National Pictures (2); Scott Manchester/Corbis Sygma; Canada Wide

SO HOW WAS THE LIFETIME MOVIE? 126-127 (clockwise from top left) Everett; NBC/Globe; Everett (3); Steve Schapiro 128-129 (clockwise from top left) NBC/Globe; Fox; USA/Everett; NBC/Globe; Everett; Craig Sjodin/ABC; Everett; Ken Sax/HBO; NBC/Globe

MYSTERIES & SUDDEN TWISTS 130-131 Randall Simons/Polaris 132-133 (from left) Zuma; Karl Gehring; Corbis Sygma; Patrick Davison/AP 134-135 (from left) Photofest; Timothy Archibald/New Times; Justin Sutcliffe/Gamma 136-137 (from left) Terry Smith; AP; Patrick Lichfield/Camera Press 138-139 (from left) Bart Ahyou/Getty; Mark Richards; Zuma; EPA 140 Dale Wittner (3) 141 (clockwise from top left) AP; Zuma; Ted Fitzgerald/AP; Express Syndication 142-143 (from left) Brian Smith/Corbis Outline; Courtesy Carol Lewis; AP

Editor Cutler Durkee **Creative Director** Rina Migliaccio **Art Director** Peter B. Cury **Photo Director** Maddy Miller **Senior Editor** Rob Howe **Writers** Steve Dougherty, Chris Strauss, Greg Adkins, Tom Gliatto, Richard Jerome, Bill Hewitt, Michelle Tan **Photo Editors** Brian Belovitch; Katherine Bourbeau **Reporters** Jane Sugden (Chief), Lindsey Bahr, Beth Perry, Charlotte Triggs, Melody Wells, Olivia Abel, David Cobb-Craig, Mary Shaughnessy, John Perra, Hugh McCarten, Ashley Williams, Lisa Kay Greissinger **Copy Editor** Alan Levine **Production Artists** Michael Aponte, Ivy Lee, Michelle Lockhart, Cynthia Miele, Daniel Neuburger

Special Thanks to Jane Bealer, Robert Britton, Sal Covarrubias, Margery Frohlinger, Charles Nelson, Susan Radlauer, Annette Rusin, Ean Sheehy, Jack Styczynski, Celine Wojtala, Patrick Yang

TIME INC. HOME ENTERTAINMENT
Publisher Richard Fraiman **Executive Director, Marketing Services** Carol Pittard **Director, Retail & Special Sales** Tom Mifsud **Marketing Director, Branded Businesses:** Swati Rao **Director, New Product Development** Peter Harper **Assistant Financial Director** Steven Sandonato **Prepress Manager** Emily Rabin **Marketing Manager:** Laura Adam **Associate Book Production Manager** Suzanne Janso **Associate Prepress Manager** Anne-Michelle Gallero **Associate Marketing Manager** Danielle Radano

Special Thanks to Bozena Bannett, Alexandra Bliss, Glenn Buonocore, Bernadette Corbie, Robert Marasco, Brooke McGuire, Jonathan Polsky, Ilene Schreider, Adriana Tierno

ISBN: 1-932994-22-X. Library of Congress Control Number: 2005902452. People Books is a trademark of Time Inc. We welcome your comments and suggestions about People Books. Please write to us at: People Books, Attention: Book Editors, PO Box 11016, Des Moines, IA 50336-1016

If you would like to order any of our hardcover Collector's Edition books, please call us at 1-800-327-6388 (Monday through Friday, 7 a.m.— 8 p.m. or Saturday, 7 a.m.— 6 p.m. Central Time).